Studien zur Mustererkennung

herausgegeben von:

Prof. Dr.-Ing. Heinrich Niemann
Prof. Dr.-Ing. Elmar Nöth

Bibliografische Information der Deutschen Nationalbibliothek

Die Deutsche Nationalbibliothek verzeichnet diese Publikation in der
Deutschen Nationalbibliografie; detaillierte bibliografische Daten sind
im Internet über http://dnb.d-nb.de abrufbar.

ISBN 978-3-8325-2446-3
ISSN 1617-0695

Logos Verlag Berlin GmbH
Comeniushof
Gubener Str. 47
10243 Berlin
Tel.: +49 030 42 85 10 90
Fax: +49 030 42 85 10 92
INTERNET: http://www.logos-verlag.de

Real World Approaches for Multilingual and Non-native Speech Recognition

Der Technischen Fakultät der
Universität Erlangen–Nürnberg

zur Erlangung des Grades

DOKTOR–INGENIEUR

vorgelegt von

Martin Raab

Erlangen — 2010

Deutscher Titel:

Praktikable Ansätze für mehrsprachige und nicht-muttersprachliche Spracherkennung

Als Dissertation genehmigt von der
Technischen Fakultät der
Universität Erlangen-Nürnberg

Tag der Einreichung:	07.10.2009
Tag der Promotion:	11.02.2010
Dekan:	Prof. Dr.-Ing. habil. R. German
Berichterstatter:	Prof. Dr.-Ing. habil. E. Nöth
	Prof. Dr. Dr.-Ing. W. Minker

Abstract

This thesis proposes a scalable architecture for multilingual speech recognition on embedded devices. In theory multiple languages can be recognized just as one language. However, current state of the art speech recognition systems are based on statistical models with many parameters. Extending such models to multiple languages requires more resources. Therefore a lot of research in the area of multilingual speech recognition has proposed techniques to reduce this need for more resources through parameter tying across languages.

After an evaluation of the previous work, this thesis was able to show that tying at the density level offers the greatest flexibility for the design of a multilingual acoustic model. Furthermore, there were also hints in the literature that densities from the native language of the speakers can be useful for the modeling of non-native accents of speakers. Based on these findings, this thesis developed an algorithm for the creation of Multilingual Weighted Codebooks (MWCs) that adds Gaussians from the spoken languages to the native language codebook (= set of Gaussians) of the speaker. A key advantage of this algorithm is that it optimally models the native language of the speaker, which is not the case for most of the previous work.

The results prove the effectiveness of the MWC algorithm, both for native and non-native speech, but the disadvantage of this algorithm is that it increases the training effort exponentially with the number of languages considered. The answer to this problem was found in projections between Gaussian spaces. These projections allow to generate multilingual models within fractions of a second from monolingual speech recognizers. Due to this, the problem of training effort was eliminated, as there is no longer the need to provide all possible acoustic models. Instead, it is possible to determine the languages that are needed on the embedded system and to generate the required acoustic model online. Of course, this large reduction in time causes a reduction in performance, but a combination of the MWC algorithm and the on-the-fly creation of new models leads to a scalable architecture that can recognize all languages with good performance. At the same time, the target resources are almost independent of the number of languages.

Finally, this thesis also compared several additional approaches for the optimal recognition of non-native accented speech. As the literature indicated, the use of the native language codebook of the speaker in the MWC algorithm already gave a significant improvement over monolingual systems. From the other tested algorithms, only the adaptation with additional non-native development data could outperform the baseline of native language codebooks.

Zusammenfassung

Diese Doktorarbeit stellt eine skalierbare Architektur für multilinguale Spracherkennung auf eingebetteten Systemen vor. Theoretisch können mehrere Sprachen
genauso erkannt werden wie eine einzige Sprache. Allerdings basieren Spracherkenner,
die dem aktuellen Stand der Technik entsprechen, auf statistischen Modellen deren
Erweiterung auf zusätzliche Sprachen ressourcenintensiv ist. Aus diesem Grund
haben die meisten vorherigen Arbeiten Techniken für eine gemeinsame Nutzung von
Parametern vorgeschlagen.

Nach Auswertung der bisherigen Arbeiten stellte sich heraus, dass eine Kombination der Ausgabewahrscheinlichkeitsverteilungen die größte Flexibilität für ein mul-
tilinguales System bietet. Zudem gab es Hinweise in der Literatur, dass Verteilungen
aus der Muttersprache eines Sprechers helfen können um fremdsprachliche Akzente
zu modellieren. Aufgrund dieser Erkenntnisse hat diese Arbeit einen Algorithmus für
multilinguale gewichtete Codebücher (MWCs) entwickelt, der Verteilungen von der
gesprochenen Sprache zu einem Codebuch der Muttersprache des aktuellen Sprechers
hinzufügt. Ein wichtiger Punkt bei diesem Ansatz ist, dass die Muttersprache des
Sprechers immer optimal modelliert wird.

Die Ergebnisse zeigen die Leistungsfähigkeit des MWC Algorithmus. Dieser Algorithmus hat allerdings den Nachteil, dass der Trainingsaufwand exponentiell mit
der Anzahl der betrachteten Sprachen steigt. Die vorgeschlagene Lösung dieses Problems sind Projektionen zwischen Funktionenräumen über Gaußkurven bei einem fixen
Codebuch. Diese Projektionen erlauben das Erzeugen multilingualer akustischer
Modelle ausgehend von einsprachigen Modellen innerhalb von Sekundenbruchteilen.
Dies löst das Trainingsproblem, da man nicht mehr alle möglichen Systeme erzeugen muss. Stattdessen ist es möglich, die benötigen Sprachen auf dem eingebetteten System zu bestimmen und die benötigten Systeme nur bei Bedarf zu erzeugen.
Selbstverständlich führt diese Aufwandsverringerung zu Leistungseinbußen, aber eine
Kombination aus dem MWC Algorithmus und der Projektion führt zu einer skalier-
baren Architektur mittels derer ein Modell ensteht, welches alle Sprachen gut erken-
nen kann. Gleichzeitig sind die benötigten Ressourcen nahezu unabhängig von der
Menge der betrachteten Sprachen.

Zuletzt hat diese Arbeit noch einige Ansätze für die verbesserte Erkennung nicht-
muttersprachlicher Äußerungen verglichen. Wie schon in der Literatur angedeutet
führte das Kombinieren von Verteilungen mehrerer Sprachen im MWC Algorithmus
zu einer signifikanten Verbesserung gegenüber einsprachigen Systemen. Von den an-
deren getesteten Verfahren konnte nur die Adaption mit nicht-muttersprachlichen
Daten eine weitere Verbesserung erzielen.

Acknowledgment

A PhD thesis is never only the work of one individual. At the beginning, there are people needed that explain the existing systems to the PhD student. In the middle, the developed ideas are refined and improved in discussions with others and at the end reviewing is needed to finally come up with something that is worth to be called a PhD thesis. In my case, these tasks were performed by the following persons.

- Dr. Rainer Gruhn

- Raymond Brückner

- Tobias Herbig

- Olaf Schreiner

- Christian Hillebrecht

- Helmut Lang

- Dr. Andreas Hagen

- Dr. Franz Gerl

- Dr. Guillermo Aradilla

- Dr. Volker Schubert

- Prof. Dr. Dr. Wolfgang Minker

- Prof. Dr. Elmar Nöth

Apart from the human support, a PhD thesis needs also financial support. For this I have to thank Harman/Becker and Nuance, that made my PhD thesis possible.

Martin Raab

Contents

Abbreviations

- ASR: Automatic Speech Recognition

- CALL: Computer Assisted Language Learning

- DCT: Discrete Cosine Transform

- EM: Expectation Maximization

- FBWA: Frequency Band Weight Adaptation

- FR: French

- G2P: Grapheme to Phoneme

- GE: German

- GMM: Gaussian Mixture Model

- GR: Greek

- HBAS: Harman/Becker Automotive Systems

- Hiwire: Human Input that Works In Real Environments

- HMM: Hidden Markov Model

- IPA: International Phonetic Alphabet

- ISLE: Interactive Spoken Language Education

- IT: Italian

- JSGF: Java Speech Grammar Format

- KLD: Kullback Leibler Divergence

- L1: native language of a speaker

- L2: spoken language OR L2 distance

- LBG: Linde-Buzo-Gray Algorithm

- LDA: Linear Discriminant Analysis

- LMC: Linear Model Combination

- LVM: Log Variance Minimization

- MAH: Mahalanobis distance

- MFCC: Mel Frequency Cepstral Coefficients

- MLLR: Maximum Likelihood Linear Regression

- MM: Model Merging

- MWC: Multilingual Weighted Codebooks

- otfMHMM: on-the-fly multilingual HMM algorithm

- PBM: Parallel Bilingual Modeling

- SP: Spanish

- US: American English

- WA: Word Accuracy

- WER: Word Error Rate

Chapter 1

Introduction

1.1 Multilingual Speech Recognition

1.1.1 Prolog

Imagine a German tourist looking forward to a wonderful holiday in Marseille, France. Imagine he is driving there with his new car with the latest, speech driven car infotainment system. Of course, he will most of the time interact with the system in German. On his way, however, he will drive through Italy and France. His holiday is long enough, so he wants to explore some cities on his way.

Apart from Milano and Cannes, he wants to tell his navigation system to drive to Rozzano, Italy and to Roquebrune-Sur-Argens, France. As these city names do not belong to the language of the user interface, current speech recognizers are not able to handle such names when they are spoken. Therefore a multilingual speech recognizer is needed in order to recognize the German commands the user will utter as well as the foreign city names.

But there are further reasons why the user would want to have a multilingual speech recognizer on his journey. For example, he prefers to listen to his own music collection rather than to radio stations in foreign languages. Even the most convenient haptic music selection systems however will distract the driver on his long way. It would be much better if it were possible to say the name of the artist, instead. But as for the city names above, many artists names are not German. Again, without multilingual speech recognition such a system is not possible.

These examples demonstrate that multilingual speech recognition is an essential feature of future car infotainment systems. But, it should not be forgotten that the user drives most of the time in one country and speaks one language. Thus, he will most of the time travel within his country, and the commands he uses will always belong to one language. Therefore, multilingual recognition is necessary, but it can not be allowed to degrade performance on the user's native language, as this is the language the user employs most of the time to interact with the system. Summarized, it can be said that future car infotainment systems should

- recognize commands and other words in the user's main language with maximum accuracy,

- but it should be possible to recognize foreign names as well as possible, because they frequently occur in music titles and street addresses.

1.1.2 Non-Native Speech Recognition

The previous section showed that multilingual speech recognition is a desirable attribute of future car infotainment systems. However, it is likely that even a perfect multilingual speech recognition system will have problems to fulfill its task. The reason is that deviations in speech occur when humans speak in foreign languages. This is generally referred to as non-native accent of the speaker.

An interesting fact is that in general humans do not have too much problems to follow other speakers with non-native accent. However, this is not true for current speech recognition technologies. These techniques are amongst others based on statistical representations of speech sounds in a language. The non-native speakers, however, introduce a new, previously unseen variation to the speech sounds. This increases wrong recognitions by the statistical models significantly. Previous work by [Tomo 01b] showed error rates that are 200% higher for Japanese non-native speakers than for native English speakers on a comparable task.

There are at least three different reasons that can cause this mismatch between human and automatic speech recognition performance

- The deviation from native speech is systematic. Humans subconsciously adapt to these modifications and can understand the speaker well after this adaptation has happened.

- The statistical speech recognition models themselves are suboptimal, meaning that they do not concentrate on the same features as humans.

- It is beyond doubt that humans have superior knowledge of semantic concepts than current computer systems. It could be that humans remove errors on the level of individual sounds with this knowledge. Of course, automatic speech recognizers perform similar post-processing of the perceived signal, but maybe their post-processing can not cope with the human world knowledge.

From a research point of view, the first reason is the most promising approach. Once the systematic deviation is identified, the recognizer performs as well as for native speech. This lead to many works that tried to identify and apply these rules. The approaches differ in the amount of knowledge they use for generation of rules. Some of them use non-native speech for the supervised extraction of the deviation, some use human knowledge, some use unsupervised adaptation and finally, some try to improve non-native speech recognition without using any non-native speech. Approaches from all areas are described in Section 3.4. While it is clear that the first approach (supervised training/adaptation) is the most promising, the last approach is the most desirable. This is due to the fact that non-native accent depends on both the native language of the speaker and the actual spoken language. Thus for n languages, n^2 different accents need to be considered. The additional effort is unlikely to be undertaken for real world applications that should support between 20 and 30 languages.

Regarding the other two aspects, it is necessary to know how much effort has already been spent in designing current speech recognition systems [Furu 07]. After a toy dog in the 1920's that barked when it's name was called, the first serious speech recognizers between 1952 and 1968 recognized digits. From 1968 to 1980, word recognition and continuous speech recognition for restricted vocabularies became possible. Around 1980, the today still dominating statistical framework for speech recognition was introduced and spread fast to many research groups. Since then, the efforts in speech recognition increased continuously, around 3500 papers about speech recognition have been presented at the International Conference on Acoustics, Speech and Signal Processing (ICASSP) from 1978 to 2006. Considering all this work, this thesis investigates how the existing framework can be extended, rather than suggesting a completely new approach.

1.1.3 Combinatoric Problem

Even when the problem of non-native speech recognition is ignored for a moment, multilingual speech recognition introduces an additional problem compared to monolingual recognition. The reason is that the statistical framework that is currently used for speech recognition requires huge amounts of parameters. As example, a state of the art recognizer easily has acoustic models for 5000 different context dependent sounds, each of them is split into three models for beginning, middle and end of the sound. All these 15,000 models are described with a Gaussian Mixture distribution with 80 Gaussians in a 40 dimensional space. This totals to around 1,000,000,000 parameters for the modeling of the acoustic sounds of one language. These parameters have to be estimated from training data, and all of these models have to be evaluated for every 10 milliseconds of a speech signal. Furthermore, this was only the acoustical modeling of speech. There are other models that also have many parameters. These numbers point out that it is not advisable to just run monolingual acoustic models in parallel, as this would further increase the requirements of the system. Instead, there should be some parameter sharing between languages to reduce the number of parameters that have to be evaluated.

There are several ways how this parameter sharing can be achieved. A first idea that was put to practice by many works in the literature (see Section 3.3) is to choose one global set of phonemes and force all languages to use them. However, a phoneme is by definition the smallest unit of a language that leads to a semantic difference in the meaning of an utterance. Thus, for different languages phonemes can have slightly different realizations, and therefore it would be better to have a more fine grained sharing of sounds across languages. However, as soon as phonemes are allowed to be different for different languages, the total number of phonemes depends on the actual languages that are considered in the recognition process. Thus, the sharing can only really happen once the languages that are needed for the recognition are known.

Section 1.1.1 additionally stated that the performance in the native language of a user is often more important than in other languages. This is nothing else than a weighting of languages. There are also cases in which this form of weighting is likely to be too inflexible. One example is a speech interface for music collections. Some collections might consist of mainly English and German music titles and one or two Italian titles. Other collections may contain mostly English and Italian. In both cases, the system should support Italian speech recognition, however, ideally, the system would assign more parameters for Italian in the second case, as in this collection Italian is more important to achieve good average performance of the speech recognition engine. Thus the weighting should be more flexible, and allow to assign weights to each of the languages.

The last paragraphs indicated that there should be parameter tying, that the parameter tying is first possible after the languages are known and that the number of parameters should be allowed to vary appropriately for multilingual speech recognition. Satisfying all these demands without constraints leads to an combinatoric explosion of the number of possible multilingual acoustic models.

1.2 Motivation and Aims

This thesis was created in a cooperation between Harman/Becker Automotive Systems (HBAS) and the Friedrich-Alexander-University of Erlangen-Nuremberg, Germany. HBAS is the leading manufacturer of high-tech car audio and car infotainment. HBAS is operating world wide with about 7500 employees. Customers are nearly all major car manufacturers, among them Audi, BMW, Daimler, Lexus, Peugeot, Porsche and many more. In 2007, HBAS systems where mostly integrated in high-class cars, though the expectation is that the future will see navigation systems, rescue systems and driver assistance systems becoming more and more integrated in all cars.

While IT-systems in cars get more sophisticated, the problem of controlling all the provided functionality is becoming worse. Systems of 2007 were already no longer controllable while driving, and exploring all functions of a navigation system takes hours. This initial study effort is likely to increase further as more and more functionality becomes available. HBAS has recognized this problem already in the mid 90's, and was at the beginning of this thesis (2007) almost the only provider of speech controlled in-car systems.

Despite the advances the speech interfaces made over the years, there were and are still open questions. One of them is the problem of multilingual and non-native speech recognition, as motivated in the first two sections of this thesis.

The following examples demonstrate the benefits that multilingual speech interfaces offer to car infotainment systems. First, it is clear that saying "I want to go from Ulm to Roquebrune-Sur-Argens" is easier and more natural than

- Press the navigation button

- Choose the address method navigation selection

- Choose the country

- Enter the city letter by letter

Another possible use of multilingual speech recognition is to allow the task "Play Michel Jackson, Billie Jean", which typically leads to the following steps,

- Press the music button

- Choose the sorting of the files (by artist, by genre, by title)

- Choose the title

to be replaced by a speech command. At first, this example looks less complicated than the address input, but the last step can include scrolling through hundreds or thousands of music titles.

When this thesis was started, Harman had already prototype systems for multilingual speech recognition. Details about these systems are given in Section 4.2. For a while, it should be enough to note that these systems had a couple of issues with room for improvement

- Reduced performance on additional languages

- The training effort increased with the number of languages squared

- There were many more systems that had to be maintained

- The system design was rather inflexible, meaning that the recognizer could not adapt to the languages that are currently needed

Given these issues, and the additional problem of non-native speech recognition the goal setting of this thesis was twofold. The first goal was to suggest techniques that improve the current multilingual system. The second goal was to analyze different techniques for non-native speech recognition and to see to what extent the deviations of non-native speakers can be modeled with different knowledge sources.

Both of these goals also imply significant academic efforts. For the first goal methods had to be analyzed that can efficiently model speech for more than one language. This includes the review of existing work and its evaluation as well as the proposal of new algorithms that might be more suitable for the described scenario. The same is true for the special case of non-native accented speech. A multitude of previous work exists, spread across different areas of research. This thesis analyzes this existing work. In addition this work also proves some of the theoretical concepts about non-native speech recognition, as for example models from the native language of speakers help to achieve significant improvements in the recognition of the non-native accented speech of these speakers.

It is important to note that this thesis is not aiming at recognizing all possible languages. This is an aim that is frequently linked to multilingual speech recognition. Instead, this thesis is interested in the creation of a system that can handle between 20-30 languages for which native training data is available.

1.3 Contributions

Multilingual Weighted Codebooks

Multilingual speech recognition poses problems for embedded in-car systems, as statistical sound models for many languages have to be evaluated. Evaluating all these models with limited resources is only possible if there is some kind of parameter sharing between them. Previous work has mostly achieved this parameter sharing on the phoneme level. Phonemes are the smallest sound units that lead to different meanings of utterances. However, previous work did also show that this level is too coarse grained. The new approach considers all these findings and offers an uncomplicated method to share parameters across languages with a given weight for each language.

Projections between GMMs

Section 1.1.1 motivated that it is a desirable attribute to have a main language of the system, and additional languages. Regarding the additional languages, it is quite important to support as many additional languages as possible. However, on the limited in-car resources, running monolingual recognizers in parallel is not possible. The Multilingual Weighted Codebook algorithm is a method to reduce to number of parameters, yet only after the actual parameter sharing is determined the system can be built. This leads to many different systems, depending on the desired sharing of parameters. A traditional generation of these systems would require huge efforts, and is likely beyond commercial interest. The projection between GMMs is a new idea to circumvent this additional effort by building only the needed system, instead of building all systems.

Scalable Architecture

Allowing weighted combinations of languages is an important feature for multilingual speech recognition. A good example are music collections that should be controlled via speech commands. Some collections might consist of mainly English and German music titles and one or two Italian titles. Other collections may contain mostly English and Italian. In both cases, the system should support Italian speech recognition, however, ideally, the system would assign more parameters for Italian in the second case, as in this collection Italian is more important to achieve good average performance of the speech recognition engine. The combination of the two previously mentioned algorithms, Multilingual Weighted Codebooks and projections between GMMs leads to a scalable architecture for multilingual speech recognition on embedded systems that allows this weighting of languages with almost no additional development effort.

Non-native Adaptation Techniques

There is a distinct difference between the goal of adapting to one non-native accent or to non-native accents in general. In the first case, it is probably appropriate to collect a small amount of in-domain data to modify the models appropriately. However, the goal of this thesis is to support recognition for hundreds of different accents. This more general goal makes it unrealistic to have appropriate data for each accent and build systems specifically for each case. Regarding the literature, by far the most work has concentrated on the more promising goal of optimizing systems when only little adaptation data is available. However, few approaches really target the second goal to modify models without appropriate training data. This thesis evaluates existing techniques for non-native adaptation and compares them to newly introduced methods. Both Model Merging from [Witt 99b] and the proposed Multilingual Weighted Codebooks can achieve significant improvements on non-native speech without non-native training data.

1.4   Outline

The fundamentals of speech recognition are introduced in Chapter 2. Chapter 3 answers the questions how non-native speakers differ from native speakers, how speech recognition works and what work was done before especially for multilingual and non-native speech recognition. Chapter 4 describes the algorithms that were used in the experiments. This includes both the baseline algorithms and the new algorithms that were developed during this thesis. Chapter 5 gives a comprehensive overview of the relevant non-native speech databases and describes the applied training and test material. Chapter 6 presents the results for all algorithms. This includes comparisons between monophones and triphones for non-native speech, experiments with Multilingual Weighted Codebooks, projections between GMMs and several adaptation techniques for non-native speech. Chapter 7 considers the findings of this thesis and suggests how they can be combined with other work to come to the next generation of speech based interfaces that are no longer limited to a single language. Chapter 8 finally summarizes the work that was presented in this thesis.

Chapter 2

Automatic Speech Recognition

2.1 Statistical Framework

The goal of a speech recognizer is to produce a transcription of a spoken utterance. However, no two pronunciations of one utterance are the same, thus machines can only determine words that are likely to have produced the acoustic signal. Therefore automatic speech recognition is the optimization problem to find the most likely word sequence W for a given acoustic signal X. According to Bayes Rule this optimization problem can be formulated as follows

$$W = argmax_{W'} P(W'|X) = argmax_{W'} \frac{P(X|W')P(W')}{p(X)} \qquad (2.1)$$

The rightmost term can be further simplified as $p(X)$ does not depend on W'.

$$W = argmax_{W'} P(X|W')P(W') \qquad (2.2)$$

$P(X|W')$ is called the acoustic model that gives the likelihood that the word sequence produced the acoustic signal and $P(W')$ is called the language model [Jura 00]. The language model is the a priori likelihood of a word string.

Moving from theory to practice, Figure 2.1 shows a typical speech recognizer architecture. The time signal wave in the top left of the figure represents the acoustic speech signal. This signal is processed to retrieve features that contain the relevant information of this wave pattern. These features are the input to the decoder, the main component of a speech recognizer. The decoder collects information from the different models shown below and searches the optimal word sequence that maximizes the overall score from all models for this given acoustic signal. Once the search

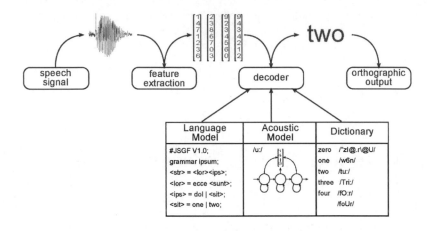

Figure 2.1: Overview of a speech recognition system

is finished, the decoder outputs the result as text. The other components deliver information to the decoder.

The acoustic model calculates $P(X|W')$, i.e. how likely it is that the wave pattern represents a certain word sequence. This is already the desired information, however, the performance of an acoustic model alone is not optimal. It is better to also consider the dictionary and the language model. The dictionary contains the words that are allowed and their pronunciation and the language model calculates likelihoods for word sequences. In the case of a JSGF Grammar [Sun 98] without probabilities as shown, the likelihood is actually reduced to an accept or reject decision. An explanation of the JSGF grammar is given later (Section 2.4). Typically the decoder can only output words in the dictionary. The correct responses from, for example, a car infotainment system are determined by a dialog system (not shown) [Mink 04]. The following sections describe each of the components in detail.

2.2 Feature Extraction

Before the speech signal can be processed by statistical models, the continuous signal has to be sampled at concrete points in time. This sampling points contain redundant information. Mel Frequency Cepstral Coefficients (MFCCs) have become the standard method for extracting the most relevant information from these samples. The most important steps for the MFCC generation are

1. Windowing: in order to obtain stationary signals that are needed for the Fourier Transform, the signal is split into 15-20ms parts. These parts are called **frames**. Each of the final feature vectors represents such a frame. The time difference between the start of two frames is called frameshift, and typically between 5 and 10ms.

2. Fourier Transform: to obtain the energy in each frequency band a Fourier Transform is applied.

3. Mel Filterbank: the Mel scale warps the input frequencies according to how humans actually perceive frequencies. In the same step, the energy over similar frequencies is averaged to reduce the number of dimensions. Typically 18 to 20 dimensions are left after this process and a logarithm is applied to them. The logarithm makes it easier to remove channel influences.

4. Cosine Transform: transforms the features back in the time domain. Allows the removal of the fundamental frequency and removes correlations in the signal. The output of this transformation is the cepstrum of the signal.

More detailed descriptions of each of these steps can be found in [Huan 01]. A figurative example of each of these steps is shown in Figure 2.2 and Figure 2.3. The picture that shows the windowed signal is less common than the other representations. It depicts the multiplication of the time signal wave with the window function in the time domain. Thus the x-axis represents the frame number and the y-axis represents the time in milliseconds within one frame. The plotted value is the result from the multiplication of the two functions. The figures are adapted from the diploma thesis of [Lang 09a] that was executed as part of the work on this thesis.

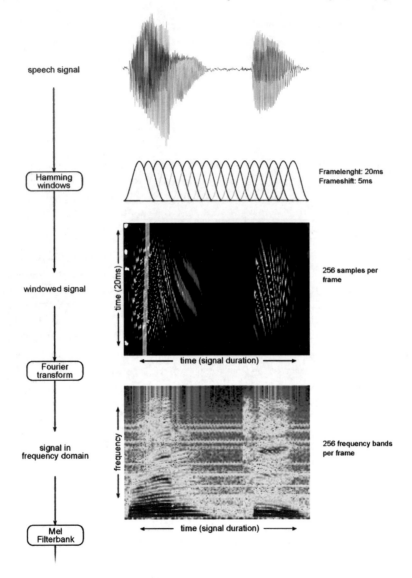

Figure 2.2: First part of MFCC computation. The waveform shown is produced by the utterance *twenty* sampled at 12800 Hz. The colored part of the speech signal has the actual size of a single 20 ms window frame. Its appearance in the windowed speech signal image is indicated by the semi-transparent gray highlighting.

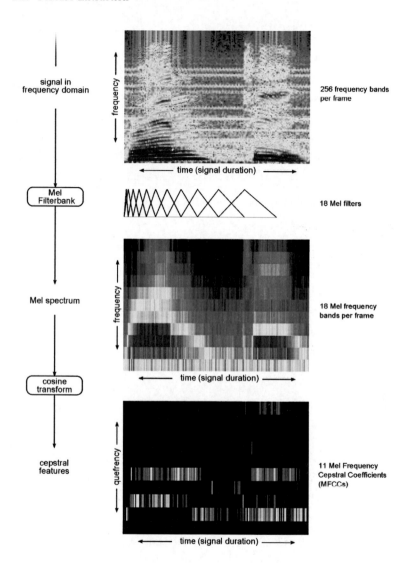

Figure 2.3: Second part of MFCC computation. The Filterbank and the cosine transform are both used for dimension reduction.

2.3   Acoustic Model

2.3.1   Hidden Markov Models

The state of the art approach for the acoustic model are Hidden Markov Models
(HMMs) [Rabi 89]. HMMs are basically weighted finite state automata that assign
probabilities to sequences of sounds. The main difference to weighted finite state
automata is that the state sequence of an HMM is never observable (it is hidden).
The concepts and algorithms described in this section are taken from [Huan 01].

Definition 2.3.1 (HMM):

An HMM is denoted by a 6-tuple

$$\boldsymbol{\theta} = (\mathbf{Q}, \mathbf{C}, \mathbf{A}, \mathbf{B}, q_1, q_N)$$

in this context is:

- $\mathbf{Q} = \{q_1, \ldots, q_N\}$ a finite set of *states*

- $\mathbf{C} \subseteq \mathbb{R}^n$ an *output alphabet*

- $\mathbf{A} = \left\{ \begin{array}{cccc} a_{11} & a_{12} & \cdots & a_{1N} \\ \vdots & & \ddots & \vdots \\ a_{N1} & & \cdots & a_{NN} \end{array} \right\}$

  a set of *transition probabilities* where a_{ij} represents the probability of a
  transition to j, when the current state is i.
  Formally: $a_{ij} = P(X_{t+1} = q_j | X_t = q_i)$, $a_{ij} \leqslant 0$, $\sum_{j=1}^{N} a_{ij} = 1$, $1 \leqslant i \leqslant N$

- $\mathbf{B} = \{b_1, b_2, \ldots b_N\}$ with $b_i : \mathbf{o}_t \mapsto P(\mathbf{o}_t)$, $\mathbf{C} \to [0,1]$, $1 < i < N$ a
  set of probability measures called *observation likelihood* that assigns each
  observation $\mathbf{o}_t \in \mathbf{C}$ a probability for being emitted by state q_i.

- $q_1 \in \mathbf{Q}$ the *start state* of the HMM. This state is non-emitting. So the
  corresponding observation likelihood $b_1(\mathbf{o}_t) = 0 \ \forall \mathbf{o}_t \in \mathbf{C}$ and the probability
  $a_{i1} := 0 \ \forall i \in \mathbf{Q}$

- $q_N \in \mathbf{Q}$ the *exit state* of the HMM. It is also non-emitting and as it is the
  final state $a_{NN} := 1$.

In these HMMs, each state has to assign a probability that it has emitted the feature vectors that are calculated from the speech signal. As these feature vectors are continuous values in $\mathbb{R}^n$ continuous valued probability functions are needed for this task. Due to their computational simplicity normal distributions are used for this purpose. To increase the modeling power, mixtures of Gaussians are used.

2.3.2 Semi-continuous Acoustic Model

On a low level, Gaussian probability distributions determine the likelihood that an incoming feature frame was generated by a HMM state. A collection of such Gaussians is called codebook. In more general systems, different sounds are allowed to have different codebooks. While this has the advantage of increased accuracy of the models it also increases the computational effort significantly. Therefore, a common method to keep the computational load feasible on an embedded system is to use only one codebook with K Gaussians for all phonemes. Each Gaussian in this codebook is described by its expected value $\boldsymbol{\mu} \in \mathbb{R}^n$ and its covariance matrix $\boldsymbol{\Sigma} \in \mathbb{R}^{n \times n}$

Thus each emitting state $q_i \in \mathbf{Q}$ has a set of K weights c_{ik}, satisfying $\sum_{k=1}^{K} c_{ik} = 1$, $1 < i < N$. The probability b_{ik} that Gaussian k emitted the feature vector $\mathbf{o}_t$ is

$$b_{ik}(\mathbf{o}_t) = \frac{1}{\sqrt{(2\pi)^n |\boldsymbol{\Sigma}_{ik}|}} \, e^{-\frac{1}{2}(\mathbf{o}_t - \boldsymbol{\mu}_{ik})' \boldsymbol{\Sigma}_{ik}^{-1} (\mathbf{o}_t - \boldsymbol{\mu}_{ik})}, \; 1 < i < N, \; 1 \leqslant i \leqslant K \qquad (2.3)$$

The likelihood b_i of emitting a feature vector $\mathbf{o}_t \in \mathbb{R}^n$ in state q_i is then:

$$b_i(\mathbf{o}_t) = \sum_{k=1}^{K} c_{ik} b_{ik}(\mathbf{o}_t) \qquad (2.4)$$

Figure 2.4 depicts such a semi continuous system. As there is only one codebook, each Gaussian can be evaluated before the decoder and only the output probabilities of the Gaussians are passed to the decoder.

2.3.3 Codebook Generation

The procedure used to find an adequate set of representative Gaussians is called *Linde-Buzo-Gray (LBG)* algorithm, which is an extension of the *k-means* algorithm [Lind 80, Huan 01].

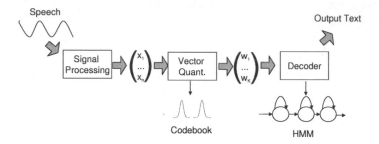

Figure 2.4: Special components in a semi-continuous acoustic model. $x_{1...n}$ are elements of the n-dimensional feature vector and $w_{1...K}$ are the weights of the K Gaussians in the codebook.

Definition 2.3.2 (LBG algorithm):

1. **Initialization** Set M=1 and find the centroid $\boldsymbol{\mu}_1$ of the whole training data. This is typically the mean vector $\boldsymbol{\mu}_1 = \frac{1}{\sum_{i=1}^{N} T_i} \sum_{i=1}^{N} \sum_{t=1}^{T_i} \mathbf{o}_{it}$ over all N observations $\mathbf{O}_1 = \{\mathbf{o}_{11}, \mathbf{o}_{12} \ldots \mathbf{o}_{1T_1}\}, \mathbf{O}_2 = \{\mathbf{o}_{21}, \mathbf{o}_{22} \ldots \mathbf{o}_{2T_2}\} \ldots$ $\mathbf{O}_N = \{\mathbf{o}_{N1}, \mathbf{o}_{N2} \ldots \mathbf{o}_{NT_N}\}$ in the training data.

2. **Split** Split each codeword $\boldsymbol{\mu}_m$, $m = 1 \ldots M$ in two points that are far apart in each partition using a heuristic method, and use these two points as the new centroids for the new $2M$ codebook. Now set $M = 2M$.

3. **Nearest-neighbor Classification** Classify each training vector $\mathbf{o}_{it}$ into one of the cells C_k by choosing the closest codeword $\boldsymbol{\mu}_k$ with ($\mathbf{o}_{it} \in C_k \iff d(\mathbf{o}_{it}, \boldsymbol{\mu}_k) \leqslant d(\mathbf{o}_{it}, \boldsymbol{\mu}_j) \; \forall k \neq j$). Where d is an appropriate distance measure between two vectors.

4. **Codebook Update** Compute the centroid of the training vectors in each cell and update the codeword $\boldsymbol{\mu}_m$ of every cell.

5. **Iteration** Repeat steps 2–4 until the number of codebook vectors is K, an a-priori designated number that obviously has to be a power of two.

After the computation of the mean values the covariance matrix Σ_k is the covariance of all training vectors in cell C_k.

2.3.4 Training Hidden Markov Models

The *Baum-Welch* algorithm (also known as Forward-Backward algorithm) is a typical method to estimate the model parameters of an HMM. It is an instance of the *Expectation-Maximization* or *EM* algorithm and – confronted with an observation sequence – iteratively increases the likelihood that the trained HMM generated the observed data. This means that given an HMM $\boldsymbol{\theta}$, with parameters initialized e. g. randomly and a training sequence $\mathbf{O}$, the HMM $\hat{\boldsymbol{\theta}}$ that is returned after the Baum-Welch algorithm, will cause that $P(\mathbf{O}|\hat{\boldsymbol{\theta}}) \geqslant P(\mathbf{O}|\boldsymbol{\theta})$. Only $\mathbf{A}$ and $\mathbf{B}$ (the transition probabilities and the observation likelihoods) of the HMM are adapted [Jura 00].

The following definitions give the essential parts that contribute to the Baum-Welch algorithm.

Definition 2.3.3 (Forward probability):

Given a sequence of observations $\mathbf{O} = \{\mathbf{o}_1, \mathbf{o}_2, \ldots, \mathbf{o}_T\}$ and a corresponding HMM $\boldsymbol{\theta} = (\mathbf{Q}, \mathbf{C}, \mathbf{A}, \mathbf{B}, q_1, q_N)$ the forward probability $\alpha_t(i)$ is defined as the probability $P(\mathbf{o}_1, \mathbf{o}_2, \ldots, \mathbf{o}_t, q_t = i|\boldsymbol{\theta})$. This is the likelihood of being in state i after seeing the first t observations.

The forward probability can be recursively calculated as follows:

Definition 2.3.4 (Forward procedure):

Initialization:
$$\alpha_1(i) = a_{1i}b_i(\mathbf{o}_1),\ 1 \leqslant i \leqslant N \tag{2.5}$$

Induction:

$$\alpha_t(j) = \left[\sum_{i=1}^{N} \alpha_{t-1}(i)a_{ij} \right] b_j(o_t),\ 1 < t \leqslant T,\ 1 \leqslant j \leqslant N, \tag{2.6}$$

Termination:
$$P(\mathbf{O}|\boldsymbol{\theta}) = \sum_{i=1}^{N} \alpha_T(i)a_{iN} \tag{2.7}$$

If $\boldsymbol{\theta}$ models a word W in language $\mathcal{L}$, $P(\mathbf{O}|\boldsymbol{\theta})$ (the probability that HMM $\boldsymbol{\theta}$ emitted $\mathbf{O}$) becomes $P(\mathbf{O}|W)$, the first part of Equation 2.1.

Definition 2.3.5 (Backward propability):

Given a sequence of observations $\mathbf{O} = \{\mathbf{o}_1, \mathbf{o}_2, \dots, \mathbf{o}_T\}$ and a corresponding HMM $\boldsymbol{\theta} = (\mathbf{Q}, \mathbf{C}, \mathbf{A}, \mathbf{B}, q_1, q_N)$ the backward probability $\beta_t(i)$ is defined as the probability $P(\mathbf{o}_{t+1}, \mathbf{o}_{t+2}, \dots, \mathbf{o}_T | q_t = i, \boldsymbol{\theta})$. This is the likelihood of seeing the remaining observations $\mathbf{o}_{t+1}, \dots \mathbf{o}_T$, when the HMM is in state i.

The backward probability can also be computed recursively:

Definition 2.3.6 (Backward procedure):

Initialization:

$$\beta_T(i) = a_{iN}, \; 1 \leqslant i \leqslant N \tag{2.8}$$

Induction:

$$\beta_t(i) = \sum_{j=1}^{N} a_{ij} b_j(\mathbf{o}_{t+1}) \beta_{t+1}(j), \; T > t \geqslant 1, \; 1 < i < N \tag{2.9}$$

Termination:

$$P(\mathbf{O}|\boldsymbol{\theta}) = \sum_{j=1}^{N} a_{1j} b_j(\mathbf{o}_1) \beta_1(j) \tag{2.10}$$

After the forward and backward probabilities for $\mathbf{O}$ are computed the parameters are adapted as follows:

- The probability $\gamma_t(i,j) = P(q_t = i, q_{t+1} = j | \mathbf{O}, \boldsymbol{\theta})$ of being in state i at time t and state j at time $t+1$, with respect to the model $\boldsymbol{\theta}$ and an observation sequence $\mathbf{O}$ is computed with:

$$\gamma_t(i,j) = \frac{\alpha_{t-1}(i) a_{ij} b_j(\mathbf{o}_t) \beta_t(j)}{P(\mathbf{O}|\boldsymbol{\theta})}, \; 1 < t \leqslant T, \; 1 \leqslant i,j \leqslant N \tag{2.11}$$

Thus for the *start* state the probability of moving to state j and observing the whole sequence is given by:

$$\gamma_1(q_1, j) = \frac{\alpha_1(j) \beta_1(j)}{P(\mathbf{O}|\boldsymbol{\theta})}, \; 1 \leqslant j \leqslant N \tag{2.12}$$

And the probability of being in state i after emitting the whole sequence and moving forward to the *exit* state is:

$$\gamma_{T+1}(i, q_N) = \frac{\alpha_T(i)a_{iN}}{P(\mathbf{O}|\boldsymbol{\theta})}, \ 1 \leqslant i \leqslant N \tag{2.13}$$

- The adapted transition probabilities are:

$$\hat{a}_{ij} = \frac{\sum_{t=1}^{T+1} \gamma_t(i, j)}{\sum_{t=1}^{T+1} \sum_{m=1}^{N} \gamma_t(i, m)}, \ 1 \leqslant i < N, \ 1 \leqslant j \leqslant N \tag{2.14}$$

That way the sum over all probabilities of being in state i and moving forward to j at any given time is computed and divided by all probabilities of being in state i and moving anywhere.

- For the adaptation of the combination weight c_{ik} a helper variable $\zeta_t(j, k)$, that expresses the probability of being in state j at time t and that the particular observation $\mathbf{o}_t$ falls into Gaussian mixture k of that state is computed:

$$\zeta_t(j, k) = \frac{\sum_{i=2}^{N-1} \alpha_{t-1}(i)a_{ij}c_{jk}b_{jk}(\mathbf{o}_t)\beta_t j}{P(\mathbf{O}|\boldsymbol{\theta})}, \ 1 < t \leqslant T, 1 < j < N, 1 \leqslant k \leqslant K \tag{2.15}$$

This has to be done separately for the start state, as there is no α_0

$$\zeta_1(j, k) = \frac{a_{1j}c_{jk}b_{jk}(\mathbf{o}_t)\beta_1(j)}{P(\mathbf{O}|\boldsymbol{\theta})} \tag{2.16}$$

- With this helper variable, the new weight c_{jk} is:

$$\hat{c}_{jk} = \frac{\sum_{t=1}^{T} \zeta_t(j, k)}{\sum_{t=1}^{T} \sum_{l=1}^{K} \zeta_t(j, l)} \tag{2.17}$$

2.3.5 Decoding with Hidden Markov Models

An efficient algorithm to compute the most probable hidden sequence of states $\mathbf{Q} = (q_1, q_2, \ldots, q_T)$ traversed through an HMM $\boldsymbol{\theta}$, when it emitted a particular visible observation sequence $\mathbf{O} = \mathbf{o}_1, \mathbf{o}_2, \ldots, \mathbf{o}_T$ is the *Viterbi algorithm*.

Definition 2.3.7 (Viterbi algorithm):

Initialization:

$$\nu_1(i) = a_{1i}b_i(\mathbf{o}_1),\ 1 < i < N \qquad (2.18)$$

$$v_1(i) = 0 \qquad (2.19)$$

Induction:

$$\nu_t(j) = \max_{1 < i < N}(\nu_{t-1}(i)a_{ij})b_j(\mathbf{o}_t),\ 1 < t \leqslant T,\ 1 < j < N \qquad (2.20)$$

$$v_1(j) = \arg\max_{1 < i < N}(\nu_{t-1}(i)a_{ij}) \qquad (2.21)$$

Termination:

$$P(\mathbf{O}, \mathbf{Q}|\boldsymbol{\theta}) = \max_{1 < i < N}(\nu_T(i)a_{iN}) \qquad (2.22)$$

$$s_T = \arg\max_{1 < i < N}(\nu_T(i)a_{iN}) \qquad (2.23)$$

Backtracking:

$$s_t = v_{t+1}(s_{t+1}),\ T > t \geqslant 1 \qquad (2.24)$$

The resulting state sequence $\mathbf{Q} = (q_1, q_2, \ldots, q_T)$ is the path through the HMM that has the highest probability of emitting $\mathbf{O}$.

While for the computation of the correct probability $P(\mathbf{O}|\boldsymbol{\theta})$ (the probability that HMM $\boldsymbol{\theta}$ generated observation sequence $\mathbf{O}$) the forward (Definition 2.3.4) or backward procedure (Definition 2.3.6) has to be employed, the probability $P(\mathbf{O}, \mathbf{Q}|\boldsymbol{\theta})$ ($\boldsymbol{\theta}$ emitted $\mathbf{O}$ with state sequence $\mathbf{Q}$) is often used as approximation for $P(\mathbf{O}|\boldsymbol{\theta})$.

2.4   Language Model

The task of a language model is to score hypotheses from the acoustic model in order to favor likely word sequences over less likely word sequences. The more general the speech recognition tasks become, the more freedom has to be allowed by the language model. For such tasks n-gram models are common that allow any sequence of words, although with a small probability [Rose 00]. However, the speech recognition tasks of this thesis are command and control oriented and thus more constrained. Therefore, context free grammars are applied. An example of such a grammar in Java Speech Grammar Format [Sun 98] is shown below.

```
#JSGF V1.0 ISO8859-1 en;
grammar com.acme.commands;
public <basicCmd> = <startPolite> <command> <endPolite>;
public <startPolite> = please | could you | oh mighty computer;
public <endPolite> = [ please | thanks | thank you ];
<command> = <action> <object>;
<action> = open | close | delete | move;
<object> = [the | a] (window | file | menu);
```

The specified grammar allows sentences like "open the window" or "please close the file". The output of the grammar is a yes/no decision, either it accepts a string, or the string is rejected. This also means that all possible sequences are equally correct, and the grammar based language model can thus not be used to rerank valid hypotheses generated by the acoustic model.

The advantage of such grammars is that they constrict the search space more than n-grams and can thus give better results. The disadvantage compared to n-grams is that only specified strings can be recognized. Such a restriction is generally too strong for the recognition of spontaneous speech, but acceptable for a command and control interface. The limited complexity of the utterances that are made in command and control scenarios also contains few possibilities for non-native grammar mistakes. Thus there is no need for special grammars for non-native speakers.

2.5 Dictionary

The last component that inputs information in the decoder is the dictionary. The dictionary specifies the allowable pronunciation of words. These pronunciations are specified in phonemes. Phonemes are the sounds that occur in the spoken language. They are defined as the smallest segmental unit of sound that can lead to a different meaning of a word or utterance. This definition directly leads to the fact that different languages contain different phonemes. A comprehensive list of known phonemes in different languages can be found in the International Phonetic Alphabet (IPA, [Lade 90]) and in the Speech Assessment Methods Phonetic Alphabet (SAMPA, [Well 08]) which is an ASCII representation of the most important phonemes from the IPA alphabet.

From an intuitive point of view the dictionary should have an important role in the adaptation to non-native speech. However, as the literature review shows, most of the works that try to add additional non-native pronunciation alternatives achieve smaller improvements than modifications of the acoustic model. The reason for this is most likely that every additional alternative increases the search space of the decoder and thus makes the recognition more difficult. Therefore the work in this thesis concentrates on modifications of the acoustic model.

2.6   Evaluation Measures

The standard measure for the automatic evaluation of speech recognizers is the Word Error Rate (WER) [Bisa 04]. The WER is defined as the number of necessary edit operations divided by the number of words (N) in a sentence. Edit operations are insertion (I), deletion (D) or substitution (S) and can be calculated via dynamic programming.

$$WER = \frac{S + I + D}{N} \times 100\%$$

In this thesis, the related Word Accuracy (WA) is used as evaluation measure. The WA is 100% - WER. The WA was preferred as it was the standard measure at Harman Becker and because it is important in commercial companies to emphasize what a system achieves, and not the errors the system makes. In the case that the algorithms made only small changes it was necessary to test the significance of the changes. The applied significance test is described in Appendix B.

Absolute changes in both WA and WER depend on the magnitude of the system performance. For example, a system with 50% WER can be improved by 10% WER, whereas it will be impossible to have the same improvement on a system that originally performed with 8% WER. For this reason, it is quite common to indicate the relative change of the performance measure. In the mentioned example, the first system improves by 20% relative WER, and the second system would achieve the same improvement if it achieved a WER of 6.4%.

Chapter 3

Related Work

3.1 Linguistics of Accents

Linguistics of accents is a research field of its own. This section does not attempt to summarize all theories and results that are available in this area. Rather it highlights some major aspects and theories regarding second language performance as they were described in more detail in [Scha 06b].

The variability of spoken language is huge, even if only speech of non-accented speakers is regarded. Noise and channel differences affect the speech signal severely. Accented speech further intensifies this problem, as everybody can tell that accented speech differs from common speech, yet there is no undisputed theory how the accented deviations can be explained. But regardless if accented or not accented speech is observed, it remains true that there is an invariance within the variation. Otherwise human listeners would not be able to understand the speech without effort.

The aim of a speech recognizer must thus be to extract this invariant core of the speech signal. The different variations can be grouped into categories. Simple forms of variation are phones that are deleted, substituted or inserted. They are simple, as only one phoneme of speech is affected by the change.

More complex variation is caused by prosody. Prosody is the rhythm, stress and intonation of speech. Prosody has influence on the fundamental frequency, the energy and the duration of speech signals. In linguistic terms, the intensity, the quantity and the intonation are changed. Changes due to prosody are more complex, as they affect many phonemes: prosody is suprasegmental. It should be noted that accent itself is also a attribute of prosody [Li 05]. The consequences of prosody for ASR are discussed in [Noth 91].

Accent can be defined as the manner and modality of speaking, as there is no real standard of speech. Decomposing and analyzing accent in elements is not straight-

23

forward, as accent is a holistic acoustical impression. In contrast to dialect, an accent changes only the sounds of a language, whereas dialects also change syntax, morphology and lexical items.

In the special case of non-native accents, non-native speakers will likely produce errors due to three different sources. Some decades ago, non-native accent was mostly regarded as partial problem of **contrastive** linguistics. The pronunciation errors are due to strong contrasts in the speaking systems of the two languages. However, these are not the only source of deviations. In his 4-level accent adaptation, [Scha 06b] states that strong accents can be explained well by this theory, however, as the speakers get better, the errors will be more based on **transfer** errors. In contradiction to contrast errors, transfer errors occur for similar sounds between the speaking systems of the two languages. The speakers have learned to articulate the new sounds, but for similar sounds, they still use the sound of their language. As the sounds are similar, others will be able to understand them, yet their pronunciation is of course different from the native sound. Finally, the **interference** causes deviations as speakers learned certain speaking patterns in their main language, and might have problems to learn new speaking patterns due to the patterns they have already learned. Interference can also be referred to as negative transfer. This last source of errors was a key argument for the support of the contrastive hypothesis, which will be described more in detail in Section 3.2.1.

It seems that there are further sources for errors, as many learners of a language make errors that are typical for native children as well. Thus, these errors are inherent to the language, and can not be based on differences between languages.

Another aspect that Schaden finds for non-native deviations is a general tendency for speakers to replace sounds that require extreme articulation positions by sounds with more moderate articulatory features. In general, articulatory features might be a helpful source of information. [Stue 03b] state that articulatory features are rather independent of the spoken language, and features can be trained with speech of one language for the recognition of another language. A further aspect is that non-native speakers are more aware of what they say, therefore their speech is more affected by distraction or emotions like fear or thinking processes.

3.2   Second Language Acquisition

This section presents four major theories of second language acquisition. The contrastive hypothesis, the identity hypothesis, the theory of learners' errors and the interlanguage hypothesis.

3.2.1 Contrastive Hypothesis

The contrastive hypothesis was formulated by [Frie 45] and [Lado 57]. Basically, the idea is that structural differences between languages cause interferences for learners that hamper the learning of the other languages. Structural similarities, however, support positive transfer and lead to correct utterances in the foreign languages.

The theory is based on a behavioristic point of view, which regards the human as a reacting system, which acquires knowledge and behavior as a reaction to the influences of his environment. Thus the second language acquisition is regarded as a process of imitation, following a stimulus reaction scheme [List 81].

Originally, the hypothesis made a **strong claim**, meaning the hypothesis can not only explain errors that learners make, but also predict errors that learners will make. The theory of learners errors (see Section 3.2.3) showed that it was not possible to hold this strong claim. After the criticism, the strong claim was replaced by a **weak claim**. The weak claim states that the interlingual transfer remains the most important source of errors for language learners, but it is also accepted that errors will occur only due to aspects of the language to be learned. Furthermore, the weak claim does no longer persist that the contrastive analysis can predict learner errors.

Consequences of the contrastive hypothesis for language learning were for example that language learning was treated as forcing the learners to strictly adapt to the speaking habits of the language to be learned. This also means that translation is not a valuable tool for learning a new language, as it is no process of imitation. Additionally, from the origins of the contrastive hypothesis, it seemed unimportant to teach the grammar of the new language, as speaking is not under the explicit control of the speakers. Today it is widely accepted that the contrastive analysis can not explain all errors that are made by beginners.

3.2.2 Identity Hypothesis

In contradiction to the behavioristic interpretation, the identity hypothesis is based on the cognitive or nativism theory of [Chom 65]. Chomsky objects the learning of language as a pure imitation process. The learners use logic and their cognitive abilities to generate sentences they did not hear before. Therefore humans must use their creativity when they learn a language.

The general belief of nativism is that humans are not born with merely physical abilities. They also have physiological abilities. Regarding speech, humans are born with the language acquisition device for learning language.

The central statement is that learning of a second language is the same as learning the mother language. The learner uses his innate ability to learn languages by listening to the language. When the learner listens to an utterance, he is analyzing the utterance and guessing rules, how this utterance might be produced. Through the iterative process of listening again and again to the language, he can build a complex system of rules, which is verified with each new utterance the learner listens to.

The identity hypothesis has lead to the idea of several sources for errors, as listed in [Mich 99]

- overgeneralization: a rule is generalized to a new category, that does not follow this rule

- simplification: a complex rule is approximated by a simple rule

- regularization: replacing irregular word forms through regular word forms, that do not exist in the language

- reduction: grammatic features that are redundant to the learner are removed

An exact categorization of errors by these types of errors is hard and not always possible. These attempts of error categorization lead to the scientific analysis of mistakes in the error analysis (see 3.2.3).

Similar as for the contrastive analysis, a **weak** and a **strong** version of the identity hypothesis exist. The strong version states that the identity hypothesis is true for all learners of a second language, whereas the weak version only states that this is true for learners learning the language in everyday use. The weak version does not refer to learners learning in an artificial class room situation.

3.2.3   Theory of Learners' Errors

The theory of learners errors, or error analysis goes back to [Cord 67]. At the beginning, error analysis was an alternative to contrastive analysis, analyzing the errors of learners and the differences between first and second languages. Through this analysis, it became clear that the strong claim of the contrastive hypothesis to predict errors did not hold true for many errors of learners.

The aim of error analysis was to categorize the errors learners make. This categorization was in many cases rather difficult, and it became clear that this does not lead to a theory that can explain all errors language learners make. Thus, while error analysis remained an important tool, it was already abandoned as a theory in the mid 1970s.

3.2.4 Interlanguage Hypothesis

Both the contrastive hypothesis and the identity hypothesis have the claim to explain and predict errors of learners of a second language. The error analysis has shown that none of them alone can explain the errors learners make.

The interlanguage hypothesis [Seli 72] states that it is truly necessary to analyze utterances of second language learners. According to this theory, each learner builds a **specific linguistic system**, that is influenced by the native and the second language, as well as attributes that are independent from native and second language. Furthermore, the linguistic systems change over time to approximate the linguistic system of the target language better. These changing linguistic systems are also referred to as approximative systems [Nems 71].

A main progress compared to the preceding hypotheses is that the interlanguage hypothesis considers linguistic as well as psycholinguistic aspects, the latter ones were not considered by the predecessors. [Baus 79] lists five different psycholinguistic processes, that affect the linguistic systems of the learners:

- Transfer from other languages: Rules and habits of mastered languages are applied for mastering the new language

- Transfer from the learning environment

- Learning strategies: the learner derives new rules, evaluates them, keeps good rules and revises wrong rules

- Strategies of communication: if words are missing, learners have to describe their communication goals, rather than using the direct way of communication

- Overgeneralization: rules become applied in similar speaking situations, although they are not valid for the new speaking situation

An unsolved problem is why adult learners tend to keep some rules in their approximative systems and do not continue the development of their approximative system until they have achieved the linguistic system of the target language. It remains an open research question, if adults have lost the ability to modify their linguistic system, or if they lack the motivation to fully adapt the target linguistic system. The effect that learners stop to develop their linguistic system is called **fossilization** [Seli 72].

As can be seen, the five aspects that affect the second language acquisition cover both the sources of errors that lead to the contrastive hypothesis as well as the identity hypothesis.

3.3   Multilingual Speech Recognition

In theory, multilingual speech recognition can be performed as monolingual speech recognition. In practice, however, different issues arise. A first question is if the required resources like dictionaries and speech training data exist for the targeted languages. A second question is if the similarities between sounds in languages can be utilized for **parameter reduction**. This means that more or less redundant calculations are removed. For example, if it is known that an English sound "a" and a German sound "a" are very similar, then it might be sufficient to calculate the probability of one of the two models, instead of both probabilities.

For the work in this thesis, the first question is more or less ignored, as the world's major languages are targeted and the necessary resources exist for these languages. The second question however is of paramount importance, as the speech recognizer eventually has to operate on embedded systems. The next section discusses further designs question that occur in the context of multilingual speech recognition to better understand how the works in the literature differ.

3.3.1   Design Questions

A perfect multilingual recognizer would recognize all languages as well as humans, need almost no resources and would not depend on any language specific resources. Of course, in practice this is currently unfeasible and decisions have to be made. Work in the literature is for example different with respect to the following aspects:

- Development resources: Are there enough resources for all languages? Is only limited material available for some languages? Are there some languages that miss some necessary information?

- Target resources: Is maximum performance allowed at all costs? How many additional parameters are allowed for each additional language?

- Language pool: How many languages are considered? Are extremely different languages in the pool?

- Parameter reduction: How is the parameter sharing achieved? Is the sharing derived manually or data driven?

- Simultaneous: Will one speaker always speak one language? Are language switches only allowed between utterances or also within one utterance?

- Priority language: Are all languages of equal importance or not?

- Non-native: Are there only native speakers? Are there only non-native speakers? Can there be both?

These differences make clear that there are few works that are comparable in all aspects. It is also true that different choices have to be made for different target scenarios. For example, for systems that only have to recognize strongly accented non-native speech and have very limited resources, context independent acoustic models might be more appropriate than for systems that have to recognize almost fluent speech and have more target resources available.

Regarding this thesis, the treatment of non-native speech is of major importance. Therefore, this topic is discussed in detail in Section 3.4. The rest of this section is categorized by the criterion of parameter reduction. Section 3.3.2 reviews the literature for algorithms that can derive phoneme similarities.

3.3.2 Phoneme Distances

For many approaches in multilingual speech recognition it is necessary to know which phonemes are similar across languages. A first approach to determine similarities of phonemes is to compare their features as described in the International Phonetic Alphabet (IPA, [Lade 90]). The advantage of this approach is that the IPA phoneme attributes are defined for many languages already, and once this information is available the process can be fully automated. The disadvantage is that there are instances in which one phoneme in a given language has no counterpart in other languages, or counterparts that fit equally well. The second aspect will especially cause problems if IPA based similarities should be extended to context dependent models.

A second approach is to measure log likelihood differences on a test set when one model was replaced by another [Juan 85]. This approach is theoretically sound and likely to give good similarity metrics for the desired application. However, this approach is quite expensive, especially as non-native speech development data for each accent would be needed.

A third approach is to recognize speech of a given language twice, once with a phoneme recognizer of this language and once with a phoneme recognizer of the other language of interest [Ande 93, Goro 01a]. A comparison of the two recognition results leads to a confusion matrix that gives probabilities for the confusion of the phonemes. These confusion probabilities can also be used as a measurement how similar two phonemes are.

In addition to these three approaches any measure that can determine distances between Gaussian Mixture Models (GMMs) can be used if two acoustic models are

available. Examples are discrete entropy distance [Huan 90], approximations to the
Kullback Leibler Divergence [Falk 95, Hers 07], the Bhattacharya Distance [Mak 96]
and the L2 Distance [Jian 05].

3.3.3   Linguistically motivated Parameter Reduction

In the majority of works the parameter reduction is achieved through a phoneme
set that is shared across languages. Such a multilingual phoneme model was first
proposed in [Dals 92]. In this paper mono- and polyphonemes are defined. Mono-
phonemes are phonemes that are specific for a given language, and polyphonemes
are phonemes that occur in more than one language. These decision are based on
phonetic features like place and manner [Lade 90].

This same idea was advanced by [Weng 97]. They share codebooks for similar
phone classes in English and Swedish. They also build bilingual language models that
allow language changes within one utterance. In their experiments, a 50% reduction
of the number of codebooks does not affect the WER, but the bilingual language
models reduce the performance on both languages. However, they do not mention
the total number of Gaussians that they used, and it could be that they attempted
to train too many Gaussians for the available data.

Another work that applied the idea of multilingual phoneme models is [Ward 98].
They work on a bilingual French English system and test a bilingual phoneme set
that adds 9 French specific phonemes to the English phoneme set. When they used
language questions in the construction of their context dependent models the performance was only little worse than monolingual systems. However, such a split
theoretically allows to get the same amount of models as in the monolingual case.
Therefore their results without these language questions are more relevant for tasks
where a large parameter reduction is needed. In this case, the performance drop was
between 10-15% relative WER.

This idea was extended to a more multilingual scenario by [Schu 99, Schu 00,
Schu 01]. A first merit of this work is the collection of a large multilingual database
(GlobalPhone) that contained initially transcribed speech for 12 languages and currently supports 17 languages [Schu 06]. With the help of this data, the multilingual
phoneme models could now also be evaluated in a true multilingual task with more
than two languages. In [Schu 01] they report the average behavior of the IPA based
models on ten languages (Croatian, Japanese, Korean, Spanish, Turkish, German,
English, Japanese, Polish, French). In their terminology, ML-sep are language dependent monolingual systems, ML-mix is a global phoneme model that models all
similar phonemes with exactly the same HMM and ML-tag is the approach that adds

language questions in the creation of context dependent models. Their results show an absolute 1.1% WER increase when same sized ML-sep and ML-tag are compared. An ML-tag system that reduces the model size by 60% increases the WER by 3.1%. A ML-mix system with the same size reduction increases the WER by 8.4% absolute compared to the ML-sep systems. These results are the averaged performance for five languages. It is likely that the performance drops further if more languages are considered.

Relatively recently the idea of multilingual phoneme models was extended to exotic languages by [Nies 06]. He reports improvements for combinations of English/Afrikaans and Xhosa/Zulu. These improvements are probably due to too few training data for each individual language, but nevertheless show that the IPA based approach can actually improve the performance in special cases.

Another interesting suggestion by Stueker [Stue 03a, Stue 03b] showed that articulatory features remain consistent across languages, and can be trained on one language and used for recognition of another language. In addition, he found that features trained on multiple languages outperform features that are trained only with data from one language. Finally, a combination of the articulatory feature recognizer with a conventional HMM based speech recognizer lead to a significant improvement over the HMM based system alone.

[Ceti 07] analyzed articulatory features for cross-language transfers. In their cross lingual experiment, the transfer of articulatory features trained on one language reduced the performance. Their conclusion was that a phone based approach is better for language transfer.

3.3.4 Data driven Parameter Reduction

Similar to the linguistically motivated approaches, the first data driven approaches to a multilingual phoneme model were performed by [Ande 93]. In this work, they obtained similar phonemes through a confusion matrix approach. They report that they could replace 8 out of 30 phonemes of the Danish phoneme set by phonemes that were only trained on English, German and Italian. For this very specific setting, the phoneme recognition of each of these eight phonemes was improved compared to a complete training of all phonemes on Danish.

[Bona 97] merged five different dissimilarity measures to one averaged measure, among them the Bhattacharya distance, an entropy loss and a common acoustic space of single Gaussian distributions. These distances were combined in such a way that they could explain the phonetic categories in Italian. The experiments were then performed with Italian, Spanish, German and English. At a parameter reduction of about 50% for the 4 languages their WA is reduced by 1.3% for English (best case) and 4.5% for German (worst case).

The confusion matrix on a test set approach was extended to context dependent models by [Impe 99]. They report initial results with single Gaussians as output distributions, but in this case their WA was reduced by 3% absolute when they decreased the parameters by 65%. Their system was tested on Slovenian, German and Spanish.

A manual evaluation of the distance measure proposed by [Juan 85] is done in [Dals 98]. They conclude that this distance comes to linguistic trustworthy results and that future language identification systems should focus more on language specific systems.

3.3.5 Comparisons of Parameter Reduction Techniques

[Uebl 01] reports results of multilingual recognition of seven languages. She shows that it is possible to train recognizers for one language without speech data for this language. This is achieved by using a phoneme mapping and using speech from other languages to train the system with this mapping. The conclusion from these experiments is that data sparseness in some languages can be overcome, but the performance can not compete with standard monolingual recognizers.

[Uebl 01] also stated that data driven phoneme maps do not lead to good results for the task described above. Furthermore [Uebl 01] presents four models for simultaneous multilingual speech recognition. From top to bottom the languages are treated more in common.

1. Language identification first, then processing by monolingual recognizers.

2. Two monolingual recognizers with shared start and end node.

3. Only one set of acoustic models, but separate language models. Thus a transition between languages is not possible.

4. Shared acoustic and language model.

In her evaluation approach 3 outperforms approach 4. In different recognition scenarios like multilingual MP3 recognition, approach 4 might be the right one, as this is the only approach which allows transitions between languages in one utterance.

[Koeh 01] compares three different methods for phoneme mapping for multilingual speech recognition. Mapping phones to the IPA alphabet, data driven clustering of phones from several languages and mapping phones to the IPA Alphabet and additionally clustering the densities of the IPA phone models. Results are reported on French, German, Italian, Portuguese, Spanish and American English. The last approach yields almost similar performance as the monolingual recognizers with 13,000 densities instead of 31,000 densities. However, the size of the monolingual systems is not specified exactly, only the number of phonemes is given. From these numbers, it is likely that the multilingual recognizer contains still 2-3 times more parameters than one of six monolingual systems alone.

The work from [Koeh 01] is different from most of the previous work as it allows to combine models at the density level. Thus it does not force complete mergers at the phoneme level. The achieved performance shows that this is the right way. The open question in this work, as mentioned by the author himself, is how well this technique will perform for context dependent models.

A recent publication that resumed the work on multilingual acoustic models is [Lin 08]. They evaluate the IPA based mappings with the KL Divergence between phonemes that are modeled by a single Gaussian. For Italian and Spanish they find three phonemes that are mapped in IPA but are actually quite different. When these three models are kept separately, small improvements are achieved on Italian tests. They also extend the decision tree clustering by starting from one root node that contains all phonemes of all languages, instead of starting from nodes that only contain context dependent models of the same center phone. This so called global decision tree built on Italian and Spanish improves the recognition on Italian test sets. An open question is how well these results can transfer to more divergent languages than Italian and Spanish.

3.4 Non-native Speech Recognition

At least eight PhD theses have already been written that deal mainly with non-native accents of speech in the context of ASR. The first one of them was written by [Arsl 96] and analyzes and suggests techniques for the classification of foreign accents of American English. The second one evaluates the use of speech recognition for computer assisted language learning [Witt 99a]. Third, [Tomo 01a] examines the recognition of non-native speech, mainly on the example of Japanese speakers of English. Fourth, [Goro 02] proposes a speaker adaptation technique for non-native speakers and a method to generate pronunciation variants without the need for non-native speech data. Fifth, [Scha 06b] derives rules for the modeling of non-native speakers. Sixth, [Bous 08] has proposed the idea of confusion based acoustic modeling discussed in Section 3.4.5. Seventh, [Tan 08] has evaluated several combinations of source and target phoneme models for Chinese and Vietnamese speakers of French. Most recently [Gruh 08] has shown that the statistical integration of pronunciation alternatives helps for non-native accented speech.

3.4.1   Design Questions

A comparison of different publications in the area of non-native speech is difficult. Each researcher evaluated on another set of data, some on databases that are not publicly available. Over the time a lot of databases have been collected (see Section 5.1.2). Of course, much research is embedded in a certain application scenario, and therefore many of the databases had to be collected. Even if there is a perfect non-native database for German accented English in a spelling scenario, another researcher might need to work on accents of Japanese. Furthermore some of the data collections are so small that they were never made publicly available.

This issue was recently at least partially ameliorated by the Human Input that Works in Real Environments (Hiwire) project [Segu 07]. Among other things, the project funded by the EC 6th Framework IST Programme made a research corpus with four different non-native accents available for interested researchers.

The Hiwire corpus [Segu 07] has attracted a lot of research, and might have the potential to become a database on which research about non-native speech recognition can be compared. Still, many researchers might need other attributes of a speech corpus for their scenario. The author believes that quite often a corpus was collected, because the researcher was not aware of the already existing and available corpora. To overcome this, the author of this thesis published an overview of available non-native databases in [Raab 07b]. An up to date online version is available at [Raab 08a]. More details about the identified corpora are presented in Chapter 5.

But this is not the only reason why it is hard to compare research in non-native speech. A categorization of algorithms and methods for non-native speech recognition in an intuitive manner is difficult due to the variety of preconditions and models they work on. Examples of these conditions are shown in Figure 3.1. Most of the conditions can be combined, thus leading to a huge variety of different preconditions and modifications which are almost unique for each technique. This issue is further intensified, as for example many lexicon adaptation techniques only work well when they are combined with other speaker adaptation techniques. This helps to reduce the search space that was increased by the added pronunciation variations.

Considering the commercial scenario in which this thesis is written, a cost intensive point is the demand for non-native data for training and adaptation. Rolling out

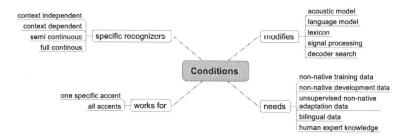

Figure 3.1: Conditions related to non-native techniques

technology requiring non-native data to a world wide market would be impossible due to the lack of sufficient training data for the various non-native accents. Consequently, the techniques are categorized according to this demand. Of course, techniques that do not need any additional training data or human effort are ideal, however, the literature review shows that such techniques can not achieve similar performance as techniques that use additional resources.

3.4.2 Recognition without Non-native Data

[Witt 99a] suggests three promising approaches for this very hard scenario. Linear Model Combination (LMC), Model Merging (MM) and Parallel Bilingual Modeling (PBM). LMC combines the Gaussian means of the native language and the spoken language and achieves up to 19% relative WER improvement. PBM combines models of the native language of the speaker (L1) and the spoken language (L2) according to a mapping, and consequently, an L2 model is represented by its corresponding L1 model whenever the L1 model has a higher acoustic likelihood. The PBM approach performes similar to the LMC approach.

Results without supervised adaptation are reported in Chapter 8 of [Witt 99a]. In the case of no adaptation, both LMC and PBM rely heavily on good initial estimates, and it will be hard to achieve similar improvements on a real test. The only technique that works consistently well even in the case of no adaptation data is MM. With MM, up to 27% relative WER improvement are achieved, and a comparable performance is achieved for many parameter values.

Combined with even very little adaptation data, all three algorithms can achieve consistent improvements. The usefulness of MM was verified by [Morg 04] on a different language pair compared to the original work by Witt. There is also a conference paper that presents these approaches [Witt 99b].

[Tan 07b] suggest amongst others a similar technique as PBM. Their results show that 'model merging' (how PBM is called in this work) performs better than acoustic model interpolation of source and target language acoustic models. The same is true for [Bart 06]. They refer to PBM as adding foreign standard units. Additionally, [Bart 06] experiment with the addition of foreign adapted HMM units instead of source language HMM models. They create foreign adapted units by adapting the target language HMM model with training data from the source language. The foreign adapted units did not help as long as they are not combined with their pronunciation adaptation.

[Tan 07b] also propose an interpolation technique for the modeling of context and language variation. This is similar to what is called model merging in this work. However, in their work, additionally models with different context lengths are merged. The results show between 6% and 16% relative WER improvement. Additional details of their interpolation approach are given in [Tan 07a]. Without the context variation, the improvement over traditional MLLR is rather small with about 5% relative WER.

[Stem 01] create a phoneme set for German accented English by training only one HMM model for both languages if the corresponding phonemes share the same IPA symbol. This approach outperforms a multilingual recognizer with both English and German phoneme models significantly. Opposed to most other work on non-native speech, this result is reported on a corpus that contains mixed German and English speech.

[Fisc 03] use ROVER [Fisc 97] and likelihood combination of multilingual HMMs for non-native digit recognition. Both approaches yield improvements for four accents of English.

[Goro 01a] generates lexicon variants as follows in a scenario with German as L1 and English as L2. German speech is recognized with a common English phoneme recognizer. In this way, English variants of the German are created. A decision tree is trained with these variants. After the decision tree has been trained, it can be applied to the German lexicon to add English variants to it. The results show that such an enriched lexicon together with MLLR outperforms MLLR alone slightly.

Another approach is Eigenvoice adaptation with some Eigenvoices being trained on the native language of the speakers [Tan 07a]. The Eigenvoice adaptation was originally proposed by [Kuhn 98]. The results are reported in a scenario with Chinese and Vietnamese speakers of French. At first a set of French Eigenvoices is trained on a French corpus. This set is then enriched with additional Eigenvoice vectors trained on Chinese and Vietnamese speech. The results verify, that the achieved improvement is not solely due to the higher overall number of Eigenvoice vectors. The improvement is roughly 5% relative WER.

As explained before, to get improvements without any non-native data is very hard, but very desirable. As the author of this work understands, even some of the above cited work uses non-native data in an indirect fashion. For example, both Witt and Morgan need a phoneme mapping. In both cases, they derived their phoneme mappings on non-native data. In theory, it is possible to derive such mappings without non-native speech. It is unclear, if such experiments can still produce comparable improvements.

How hard it is to achieve improvements can also be seen in publications that report no improvements in the absence of non-native data for training or adaptation. [Tomo 01a] describes several experiments with source language data without significant improvements. For example, the conventional adaptation methods like MAP and MLLR did not help for the Japanese speakers of English scenario. The same was true for linguistically motivated lexicon variants and Polyphone Decision Tree Specialization (PDTS). [Wang 03] state that bilingual phone models do not help in a German/English scenario. [Tran 99] come to the conclusion that an L1 Grapheme to Phoneme conversion (G2P) does in many cases not lead to an L1 accented pronunciation of L2 words.

3.4.3 Adaptation with Phonetic Knowledge and Human Expertise

Of course, all modifications to speech recognizers are based on human knowledge and intuition. This section concentrates on techniques that make modifications which need intensive human work to produce the required resources. A good example for such an approach is a rule based pronunciation adaptation, in which the rules are generated manually. Humans that experience non-native speech will have an intuition how to construct rules, but the effort to create rules that cover large parts of pronunciation errors is high. In contrast, an approach using an IPA phoneme mapping does not belong to this section, as the IPA table exists already and the effort of creating a phoneme map based on IPA should be rather moderate.

Example works for the above described manual creation of rules for lexicon adaptation are [Goro 01b], [Scha 06b] and [Bart 06]. [Goro 01b] and [Bart 06] both showed improvements with their handcrafted rules. Furthermore, both combined the lexicon adaptation with other techniques. [Goro 01b] showed additional improvements when her new lexicon was combined with MLLR and [Bart 06] reported additional improvements with foreign units and foreign adapted units. However, from the publications it is hard to give absolute numbers for the improvements.

[Scha 06b] did not evaluate his changed lexicon in a speech recognizer. Instead, he compared his pronunciation alternatives with an elaborated technique to pronunciations actually produced by non-natives. Overall, his alternatives cover the actual pronunciations in many L1-L2 pairs better than canonical transcriptions. It remains an open question if this would lead to improved speech recognition performance.

3.4.4   Supervised Adaptation with Non-native Data

[Stei 04] interpolate target language HMMs with each other. The interpolations are estimated on non-native data with the EM algorithm. An HMM is interpolated with another HMM, this is repeated for all HMM combinations. For each interpolation, the value of the maximization function is estimated. Finally, the interpolation that achieved the best score is actually performed. The HMM interpolation achieves a 6% relative WER improvement. Further improvements were achieved with an LM build on non-native speech and LM interpolation. Together, both approaches lead to a 12% relative WER improvement.

[Amda 00] modified the lexicon with pronunciation rules derived from non-native data. Their approach differs from more traditional approaches as they try to keep the amount of added variants small to guarantee that the performance of non-accented speech does not suffer. However, the improvements are only 3% relative WER.

The previously already mentioned techniques by [Witt 99a] (LMC, MM) can also be combined with supervised online adaptation. In this case, both produce consistently good results.

[Nguy 99] experiment with several different techniques for supervised and unsupervised adaptation. Results of supervised MAP and MLLR give about 10% relative WER improvement. They describe an n-best based unsupervised adaptation based on the EM algorithm, however the improvements are marginal. For supervised adaptation their n-best based adaptation achieves good results for letter recognition.

[Tomo 01a] compared many different approaches for adaptation and retraining of the acoustic model as well as modifications of the lexicon. She evaluates mainly on Japanese accented English. Even when she used non-native development data, her lexicon modification did not lead to improved performance. This shows how difficult it is to achieve improvements through modification of the lexicon. Most of the modifications to the acoustic model worked. The different approaches and their performance are given in Table 3.1.

Baseline	63.1%
PDTS	60.3%
MLLR-3	58.1%
MLLR-15	54.2%
Rebuild-L2	53.6%
MAP-15	51.7%
Retrain	48.1%
Retrain & Interpolation	45.1%

Table 3.1: Acoustic model modifications of Tomokiyo and their WER.

The baseline from [Tomo 01a] already uses unsupervised MLLR. Altogether, her whole adaptation data set size was 3 hours. PDTS is polyphone decision tree specialization with non-native data. MLLR-3 means adaption with L2 data from three speakers, and MLLR-15 with data from 15 speakers. The Rebuild system is build from scratch on the original data as well as the three hours of the accented data. The Retrain system takes the existing models and performs three EM iterations with the accented adaptation data. As this might lead to overfitting, the last system interpolates the retrained models with the original models and achieves 45.1% WER. This is a 29% relative WER reduction with 3 hours of adaptation data.

3.4.5 Training with Non-native Data

Training all components of a recognizer is in most scenarios not possible due to a lack of in-domain training data. Yet, over the time some databases (see also Chapter 5) with non-native speech have been recorded. This gives the opportunity to train at least some components partly or completely on non-native data.

An intuitive idea is to change the lexicon with the variants that are included in a non-native database. Such an approach is followed by [Gruh 04b], [Teix 97], [Tran 99], [Bode 07] and [Kim 07]. The exact methods to derive additional variants vary.

[Gruh 04b] suggest a statistical lexicon for non-native speech recognition. For each word an HMM models the pronunciation variants. The HMMs are trained with the phonetic transcription that was obtained with a phoneme recognizer. These pronunciation HMMs are used for rescoring an n-best list with the additional input of a phoneme recognizer. The rescoring obtained a consistent improvement of accented English with five different accents. [Tran 99] analyzed French subjects speaking German and derived rules based on the ONOMASTIC interlanguage lexicon [Onom 95]. For an excluded test set a large percentage of pronunciations was correctly described. The approach of [Teix 97] trains acoustic word models on non-native speech. Judging the improvements they achieve with their lexical adaptation is hard, as a table has to be compared to a chart to see the improvements. [Bode 07] achieve very good performance for the task of named entity pronunciation with finite state transducers for the generation of the pronunciations. Their work puts special focus on the pruning of variants and outperforms G2P by over 70% relative WER for named entity recognition. [Kim 07] can improve recognition of Korean spoken by Chinese speakers by 18.5% relative WER with rule based lexicon adaptation. Their rules are generated with a decision tree trained on phoneme confusion retrieved from phoneme recognition. In addition to non-native speech, the development database of both [Bode 07] and [Kim 07] contains hand made phonetic transcriptions. This makes it hard to apply their methods to more general applications.

While most research focuses on the adaptation to one non-native accent at a time, there are also works that try to adapt to non-native speech in general. [Live 99] finds that non-native speech has higher perplexity scores than native speech, but these differences do not cause a significant part of the different WER on native and non-native tests. With a finite state machine as pronunciation lexicon and acoustic model interpolation she is able to achieve 12% WER reduction. Again, this improvement is on all accents in the database, and not only for one accent.

A comparison of performance when adapting to one accent or to all accents is given in [Teix 97]. They evaluate on six different accents of English, both with word models and phoneme models. Their results with phoneme models are shown in Figure 3.2. The y-axis is the word recognition score, the x-axis shows the number of observation mixtures used for the models. The set of charts shows the performance of phoneme models, in the original work referred to as sub-word models.

Lines within one chart show the performance for Danish, German, British, Spanish, Italian and Portuguese accent. This is the same order of languages as in the chart legend to the right of each chart. Training with only native data leads to roughly 50% recognition. A training with specific accents leads to about 80%. However, the last experiment with training with data from all accents performs significantly worse and achieves only 60% word recognition score.

There is also work on the supervised adaptation of acoustic models. [Witt 99a] reports results with MM and LMC performed in combination with supervised adaptation. The improvement of LMC together with MLLR over MLLR is only marginal. However, model merging can outperform MLLR based adaptation by 24% relative WER. [Yi 06] achieve about 25% relative WER improvement on Cantonese and Wu accent of Chinese, without losing performance on standard Mandarin. They use a subword recogniser based on initials and finals of words. Their approach is to add accent specific subwords based on the accented training data. These accent specific

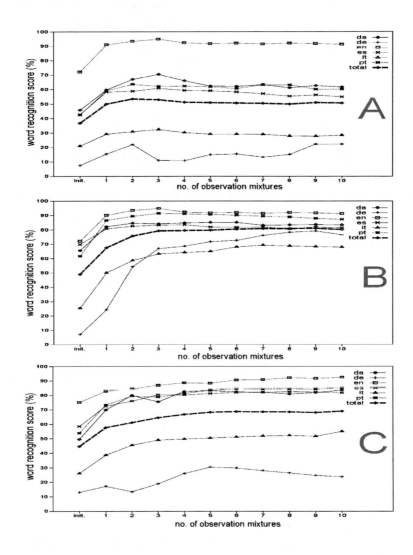

Figure 3.2: Word recognition adapted from [Teix 97]. Chart A shows the performance if only native English is used for training. Chart B the performance, when the recognizer is trained with the specific accent of the test, and the Chart C the performance when a recognizer is trained with data from all accents. The last entry in the legend indicates the average performance over all six languages.

units are integrated in the acoustic model by auxiliary decision trees. They do not change the model estimation and decoding steps. They compare their results to MAP adaptation, and can achieve about the same improvements as MAP adaptation. However, MAP adaptation had a significant negative effect on the Mandarin performance.

[Bous 05] report results about acoustic model integration, which is similar to PBM. They replace an English HMM by a combination of weighted HMMs based on phoneme transcriptions of non-native data with phoneme recognizers of both source and target language. For their experiments, the Hiwire [Segu 07] database is used. In this first publication, they achieve about 30% relative WER improvement over MLLR alone for English with French accent. In [Bous 06b] they extended their approach with additional graphemic constraints and show results for English with four different accents. The graphemic constraints improve the performance only slightly, and only for word loop grammars. The application of the acoustic model integration on the different accents gives up to 50% relative WER improvement. Similar results are reported in [Bous 06a]. In their latest publication to this topic [Bous 07], they experiment with a variety of initial HMM sets which are combined through phoentic confusion. The different HMM sets are canonical L1, canonical L2, MAP adapted versions of L1 and L2, MLLR adapted versions of L1 and L2 and retrained version of L1 and L2. Finally, they come to the conclusion that their version of PBM works best when canonical English HMMs get additional state paths from English HMMs that have been retrained with the adaptation data. This result suggests that using native models for a PBM technique is not optimal when adaptation data is available. With the best setting, they achieve around **70% relative WER** reduction. However, such a tremendous improvement is probably only achievable if enough material from the actual test speakers is available for the performed adaptations.

3.5   Summary

Section 3.1 discussed the attributes of non-native speech from a linguistic viewpoint. The review showed that while there are individual elements of speech that are modified by accents, accents can not easily be decomposed in single attributes. It is a holistic impression, and prosody changes as well as sound changes are typical features that accompany accented speech. In contrast to the common opinion that pronunciation mistakes of non-native speakers are solely caused by their mother language, this section also revealed that some errors are also typical for native children and independent of the process of acquiring a second language.

Nevertheless, the acquirement of a second language is a good start for the analysis where non-native pronunciation errors come from. Section 3.2 discussed the corresponding theories. The contrastive analysis bases on the idea that the most different sounds in new languages are pronounced wrongly. The identity hypothesis criticizes this idea, and argues for the fact that the acquirement of the new language is similar to the learning of the native language. Thus there are mostly logical errors like overgeneralization or simplification. The theory of learners errors also criticized the claim of the contrastive analysis to be able to predict errors of language learners. However, the pure analysis of errors did not lead to a coherent theory, and was thus abandoned as a theory. The newest theory, the interlanguage hypothesis is influenced by both the contrastive analysis and the identity hypothesis. However, it has reduced its goal to explain errors.

After these general discussion of multilingual and non-native speech, the next two sections discussed the technical issues of speech recognition. Section 3.3 analyzed the issues and solutions that have been proposed for multilingual speech recognition. In the beginning the different design questions that can affect multilingual systems are discussed. The rest of this section is sorted according to how the parameter reduction is achieved. At first, linguistically motivated parameter tying was developed. The review shows that a pure linguistic parameter tying leads to suboptimal performance. Therefore, data driven approaches have been developed. A combination of linguistic knowledge and data driven algorithms by [Koeh 01] achieved the best performance. The novelty of this approach is that it ties acoustic models at the density level.

Section 3.4 finally analyzed the literature of non-native speech recognition. As before, a categorization of the work in non-native speech recognition is quite difficult, as there are techniques that modify different parts of the recognizers, work on different languages or need additional training resources. In this thesis, the need for additional resources was regarded to be the most important aspect. Therefore, the section was organized according to the amount of non-native speech data needed for the generation of the models. Most of the techniques that can achieve improvements in the hardest scenario of no additional resources are based on the idea of merging source and target language models. Such algorithms reported up to 27% relative WER improvement. The other subsections then steadily improve the performance, but are less relevant for this thesis as the required additional resources are not available for a large number of target languages.

This thesis draws three main conclusions from this review:

1. Tying acoustic models at the density level outperforms tying at the phoneme level

2. The most promising techniques for non-native speech recognition without additional non-native data combine HMM models for source and target language to a new HMM model that contains densities from both languages

3. There is no work in the literature that has the same design goals as the desired system should have

The reason for point three is that there was no work identified that targeted the goal to keep monolingual performance in one language.

Chapter 4

Algorithm Description

4.1 Benchmark System

The HBAS recognizer is a semi-continuous HMM based speech recognizer as described in Section 2.3.2. The language models in the experiments are JSGF grammars [Sun 98], see also Section 2.4. The following steps have been conducted to train a monolingual speech recognizer in the reported experiments. Such monolingual systems should give optimal performance for each language, therefore each monolingual system is also the benchmark system for the respective language.

1. Generate MFCC-based feature vectors from training data

2. Create a codebook for the semi-continuous system

3. Perform vector quantization with the found Gaussians

4. Train HMMs with Baum-Welch, as described in Section 2.3.4

5. Cluster states

6. For each of the states above, train a new Gaussian by all feature vectors which belong to the corresponding state. The new Gaussians are based on the concatenation of several frames to capture dynamic effects.

7. Reduce dimensions with a Linear Discriminant Analysis (LDA)

8. Train HMMs of final classifier with 1024 Gaussians

The first six steps are used to determine a codebook for the final recognizer. Thus it was only necessary to repeat step 7 and step 8 for most of the following experiments.

4.2   Baseline System

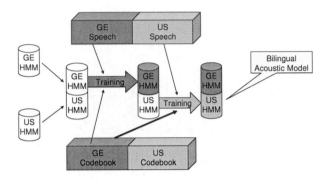

Figure 4.1: Training a multilingual acoustic model

The training process of a multilingual acoustic model, respectively a multilingual recognizer can be regarded as a concatenation of training multiple bilingual recognizers. Initially there is one main language (L1) and one additional language (L2) of the desired bilingual recognizer. Once a recognizer has been trained for these two languages, the resulting recognizer can be treated as recognizer of the "main" language (though this main language is now actually a combination of two languages). To this new main language an additional language can be added as before, thus resulting in a trilingual recognizer. It is straightforward how this concept can be extended to generate a multilingual recognizer.

The training of a bilingual recognizer is shown in Figure 4.1 at the example of training a recognizer with main language German and additional language English. At first, untrained acoustic models of the German and English are concatenated to a new bilingual acoustic model. The next step is to train the German part of the model with German speech. Then the English part of the model is trained with English speech.

An important aspect to note is that the training of the bilingual recognizer is only able to refer to one codebook. In the baseline systems this is the codebook of the main language. Experiments showed that using a German codebook for English recognition reduced the WA significantly. This issue is discussed more in detail in Section 4.3.

4.3 Multilingual Weighted Codebook

4.3.1 Motivation

From a theoretic point of view a codebook can be regarded as a collection of densities that describe the acoustic space of a language. The literature has shown that a combination of knowledge about L1 and L2 can help to recognize L1 accented L2 speech. A possible explanation for this is that the acoustic spaces of the two languages differ. Thus, using only one monolingual codebook for the recognition of multiple languages will inevitably reduce the performance. As the HBAS multilingual recognizer can only use one codebook, the need for a codebook that covers multiple languages well arises.

The standard codebook generation in the training of semi-continuous speech recognizers is not optimal for this case. The LBG algorithm that generates the codebooks (see Section 2.3.3) finds a limited number of Gaussian prototypes in the feature space that cover the training data as well as possible. In a multilingual scenario two options are possible. Either only the main language training data is provided to the LBG algorithm, or data from all languages is provided.

In the first case the codebook only covers the acoustic space of the main language. This leads to vector quantization errors for sounds that are not represented. In the second case the codebook is optimized for all languages without prioritizing the main language, thus the whole acoustic space is covered. However, in this case there is no deliberate control of the representation of the acoustic space of the main language. This can lead to performance drops in the main language. Therefore, an algorithm is proposed that keeps the knowledge about the different acoustic spaces of the different languages and can combine them appropriately.

The ideas of this section were published with an evolving set of experiments in [Raab 08b, Raab 08c, Raab 08d].

4.3.2 MWC Algorithm

A prerequisite for the Multilingual Weighted Codebook (MWC) algorithm is a codebook for each language. These codebooks are build with soft vector quantization based on the LBG approach (see Section 4.1). From these initial codebooks a new codebook is created. As this new codebook is based on codebooks from many languages, it is called multilingual, and as the influence (namely the number of codebook vectors) of each original codebook can be adjusted, it is called weighted.

To achieve the first priority aim of keeping the main language accuracy, the created MWCs always contain all Gaussians from the main language codebook. Furthermore, the Gaussians that originate from the main language are never modified. To improve the performance on the additional languages, the MWCs contains some Gaussians which originate from codebooks from the additional languages.

Thus the MWC is basically the main language codebook plus some additional Gaussians. Figure 4.2 depicts an example for the extension of a codebook to cover an additional language. From left to right one iteration of the generation of MWCs is represented in a simplified two dimensional vector space.

The picture to the left shows the initial situation. The X's are mean vectors from the main language codebook, and the area that is roughly covered by them is indicated by the dotted line. Additionally, the numbered O's are mean vectors from the second language codebook. Supposing that both X's and O's are optimal for the language they were created for, it is clear that the second language contains sound patterns that are not typical for the first language (O's 1,2 and 3).

The middle picture shows the distance calculation. For each of the second language codebook vectors, the nearest neighbor among the main language Gaussians is determined. These nearest neighbor connections are indicated by the dotted lines.

The right picture presents the outcome of one iteration. From each of the nearest neighbor connections, the largest one was chosen as this is obviously the mean vector which causes the largest vector quantization error. In the pictures, this is O number 2. Thus the Gaussians from O number 2 was added to the main language codebook.

The iteration described above will already lead to a reduced vector quantization error for utterances from the second language. Further iterations can further minimize this error.

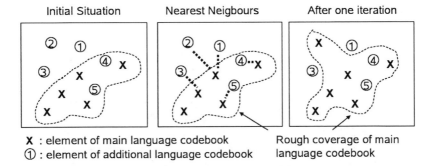

Figure 4.2: Basic idea of Multilingual Weighted Codebooks

When more than two language are considered, a first step builds a large codebook that contains all Gaussians from all additional languages. With this large codebook, the algorithm can be performed as described above. A key element in this algorithm is the distance measure between Gaussians. Different distance measures are proposed in the next section.

4.3.3 Distance Measures

Definitions

For the next sections the following definitions are needed. A and B are two n-dimensional Gaussians. Each one has a mean value $\boldsymbol{\mu}$ and a covariance matrix $\boldsymbol{\Sigma}$. Merging these two Gaussians to a new one will result in a new Gaussian C. The elements of the covariance matrices are denoted by $x_{i,j}$, where x stands for the lowercase letter of the corresponding Gaussian. The number of training samples is denoted with w for weight.

Merging

When merging two Gaussians, these two are replaced by one Gaussian that would have been estimated from all the training samples that led to the estimation of the two original Gaussians. This can be done without the need to actually know all the training samples.

The mean of the resulting Gaussian C is defined by μ_c.

$$\boldsymbol{\mu}_c = \frac{w_A\boldsymbol{\mu}_A + w_B\boldsymbol{\mu}_B}{w_A + w_B} \tag{4.1}$$

The covariance $c_{i,j}$ is

$$c_{i,j} \stackrel{\text{def}}{=} E_C(X_iX_j) - E_C(X_i)E_C(X_j) \tag{4.2}$$

where i is the row index and j the column index in the covariance matrix of Gaussian C. E_A, E_B and E_C are the expected values of the feature variable X given the training data of Gaussian A, B and C. By definition $E_A(X)$ is μ_A, the same is true for $E_B(X)$ and $E_C(X)$. Thus Equation 4.1 can be applied to replace the mean values $E_C(*)$ that have seen all training data of both Gaussians.

$$c_{i,j} = \frac{w_A}{w_A + w_B}E_A(X_iX_j) + \frac{w_B}{w_A + w_B}E_B(X_iX_j)$$
$$- \frac{1}{w_A + w_B}(w_A\mu_{A_i} + w_B\mu_{B_i})\frac{1}{w_A + w_B}(w_A\mu_{A_j} + w_B\mu_{B_j}) \tag{4.3}$$

The unknown variables $E_A(X_i X_j)$ and $E_B(X_i X_j)$ can be replaced with the help of Equation 4.2.

$$c_{i,j} = \frac{w_A}{w_A + w_B}(a_{i,j} + \mu_{A_i}\mu_{A_j}) + \frac{w_B}{w_A + w_B}(b_{i,j} + \mu_{B_i}\mu_{B_j}) \tag{4.4}$$
$$- \frac{1}{(w_A + w_B)^2}(w_A\mu_{A_i} + w_B\mu_{B_i})(w_A\mu_{A_j} + w_B\mu_{B_j})$$

$$= \frac{1}{w_A + w_B}(w_A a_{i,j} + w_B b_{i,j} + w_A\mu_{A_i}\mu_{A_j} + w_B\mu_{B_i}\mu_{B_j} \tag{4.5}$$
$$- \frac{1}{(w_A + w_B)}(w_A\mu_{A_i} + w_B\mu_{B_i})(w_A\mu_{A_j} + w_B\mu_{B_j})$$

$$= \frac{1}{w_A + w_B}(w_A a_{i,j} + w_B b_{i,j} + \frac{1}{w_A + w_B}[w_A^2\mu_{A_i}\mu_{A_j} + w_A w_B\mu_{A_i}\mu_{A_j} \tag{4.6}$$
$$+ w_A w_B\mu_{B_i}\mu_{B_j} + w_B^2\mu_{B_i}\mu_{B_j} - (w_A\mu_{A_i} + w_B\mu_{B_i})(w_A\mu_{A_j} + w_B\mu_{B_j})]$$

$$= \frac{w_A a_{i,j} + w_B b_{i,j} + \frac{w_A w_B}{w_A + w_B}(\mu_{A_i} - \mu_{B_i})(\mu_{A_j} - \mu_{B_j})}{w_A + w_B} \tag{4.7}$$

Of course, this formula could be used within the MWC algorithm to merge some Gaussians. However, it was not employed in the experiments in this thesis. This formula is only presented as motivation for the next distance.

Log Likelihood Distance

The first chosen distance measure [Xu 98] tries to minimize the gain in variance, which will always result when two Gaussians are merged to one. Looking again at the result of a merging of two Gaussians, one can see that the variance v of the new Gaussian in dimension i equals

$$v(i) = \frac{w_A a_{i,i} + w_B b_{i,i} + \frac{w_A w_B}{w_A + w_B}(\boldsymbol{\mu}_{A_i} - \boldsymbol{\mu}_{B_i})^2}{w_A + w_B}$$

The distance between two Gaussians A and B is calculated as follows

$$D_{LogL}(A, B) = \sum_{i=0}^{n} ln(v_C(i)) - \frac{w_A}{w_A + w_B}ln(v_A(i)) - \frac{w_B}{w_A + w_B}ln(v_B(i))$$

Symmetric Mahalanobis Distance

The Mahalanobis Distance [Maha 36] is a well known similarity measure between two random vectors with the same covariance matrix. The formal definition of the distance between a vector $\mathbf{x}$ and a Gaussian A with covariance matrix $\boldsymbol{\Sigma}$ and mean $\boldsymbol{\mu}$ is

$$D_M(\mathbf{x}, A) = \sqrt{(\mathbf{x} - \boldsymbol{\mu})^T \boldsymbol{\Sigma}^{-1}(\mathbf{x} - \boldsymbol{\mu})}$$

However here the distance between two Gaussians is needed. This problem is solved with the following symmetric extension of the Mahalanobis Distance.

$$D_M(A, B) = \sqrt{(\boldsymbol{\mu}_A - \boldsymbol{\mu}_B)^T \boldsymbol{\Sigma}_B^{-1} (\boldsymbol{\mu}_A - \boldsymbol{\mu}_B)} + \sqrt{(\boldsymbol{\mu}_B - \boldsymbol{\mu}_A)^T \boldsymbol{\Sigma}_A^{-1} (\boldsymbol{\mu}_B - \boldsymbol{\mu}_A)}$$

Symmetric Kullback Leibler Distance

The Kullback Leibler Divergence (KLD) is a similarity measure between two probability density functions [Kull 51]. The KLD between A and B with probability density functions a and b equals

$$KLD(A, B) = \int_{-\infty}^{\infty} a(\mathbf{x}) log \frac{a(\mathbf{x})}{b(\mathbf{x})} d\mathbf{x}$$

Similarly to the Mahalanobis Distance, this divergence metric is asymmetric. The symmetric metric which is used as distance metric based on the KLD measure is defined

$$D_{KL}(A, B) = \int_{-\infty}^{\infty} a(\mathbf{x}) log \frac{a(\mathbf{x})}{b(\mathbf{x})} d\mathbf{x} + \int_{-\infty}^{\infty} b(\mathbf{x}) log \frac{b(\mathbf{x})}{a(\mathbf{x})} d\mathbf{x}$$

The calculation of these integrals is not straightforward. According to [Camp 97, pg. 1449] $D_{KL}(A, B)$ can be calculated according to

$$D_{KL}(A, B) = \frac{1}{2} tr[(\boldsymbol{\Sigma}_A - \boldsymbol{\Sigma}_B)(\boldsymbol{\Sigma}_B^{-1} - \boldsymbol{\Sigma}_A^{-1})] + \frac{1}{2} tr[(\boldsymbol{\Sigma}_A^{-1} + \boldsymbol{\Sigma}_B^{-1})\boldsymbol{\delta}\boldsymbol{\delta}^T]$$

where tr is the trace of the covariance matrix and $\boldsymbol{\delta}$ is the difference between $\boldsymbol{\mu}_A$ and $\boldsymbol{\mu}_B$.

A point of frequent discussions during presentations of the idea of MWCs was the relationship between the last two distance measures. They are not the same. The Kullback Leibler Divergence between two Gaussians reduces to the Mahalanobis distance when the Gaussians have the same covariance. There is no simple relation between the distances when the covariances are different.

4.3.4 Simplifications

The true potential of MWCs lies in the combination of more than two languages. Making experiments with this variety of languages results in an exponentially increased training effort if the training is executed as usual. One reason for this is that the Linear Discriminant Analysis (LDA) is usually different for every set of Gaussians. In the common training approach (see Section 4.1) this LDA is generated on the codebook and the codebook itself is depending on the languages the recognizer is built for.

As a result, training a four-lingual and a five-lingual recognizer, where both systems only differ by one language needs the training of 9 languages. Comparing the five-lingual system to the four possible four-lingual systems results in the training of 21 languages. An idea to overcome this is to build the LDA on the main language part and then reapply this LDA for all additional codebooks. This allows the combination of bilingual systems to multilingual systems, as they all use the same LDA. Thus comparing a five-lingual system to all its four-lingual parts would only need the training of 5 languages, and not the training of 21 languages.

In the experimental section, results are presented for five languages, and each language was allowed to have 100 additional Gaussians. Thus the five-lingual system will have 1424 Gaussians, as it contains all Gaussians that were used for the training of all five languages.

To be able to apply the idea of LDA reload, two modifications had to be made. First, the main language LDA had to be applied for each training of an additional language. Second, in order to be able to combine the several trained additional language HMMs, their output probability matrix had to be changed.

These modifications lead to a fragmentation of the probabilities in the output probability matrix of the HMM states. This is visualized in Figure 4.3. Overall 400 Gaussians are added to the codebook, but for the five-lingual system many of them will have a weight of 0 for HMMs.

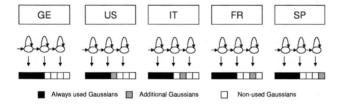

Figure 4.3: Codebook fragmentation with LDA reload. The rectangle below the HMMs represents the codebook. The black colored part are the main language Gaussians, they are always used. The four smaller rectangles are 100 Gaussians, each block was generated in a bilingual setup. As a consequence, in the shown five-lingual case, in fact only 100 additional Gaussians are used for each additional language.

The experiments in Section 6.2.3 will show that a system that is trained without this simplification is significantly better. Therefore, all other experiments in this thesis are done without the simplification proposed in this section.

4.4 On-the-fly Generation of Multilingual HMMs

4.4.1 Motivation

Section 4.3 has presented an approach to limit the number of Gaussians in the acoustic model. This solves the problem of too many parameters that have to be evaluated for every frame of speech during decoding. However, the training complexity is actually increased with this approach, as the generated acoustic models now depend on the combination of languages.

This is due to the fact that each language contributes to the common codebook, and only after a codebook is fixed HMM models can be trained. In fact, the training complexity increases exponentially with the number of languages considered with an MWC system. A key issue is that there is no straightforward way how the trained monolingual recognizers can be combined efficiently, meaning that there is parameter sharing between the models of different languages. As a consequence, the MWC approach alone is better suited for scenarios in which a rather limited set of languages is needed. For many languages, the conventional HMM training effort is too high.

Therefore this section proposes methods that can create multilingual HMMs faster. The basic idea of these algorithms relies on the facts that the only difference between multilingual and monolingual recognizers at HBAS are a different set of Gaussians, and that the training material and the HMMs for each language are the same. Thus, instead of the common iterative trainings, it is sufficient to define a projection of a GMM that is defined on one set of Gaussians to another set of Gaussians.

These projections should have two attributes. First, they have to create GMMs on the new set of Gaussians that model speech signals well. Second, the motivation is to be faster than a traditional HMM training, thus they also have to be fast. In fact, it would be very desirable to have an algorithm that can run on an embedded system. With such an algorithm, the multilingual acoustic models can be created on the embedded system itself, and there is no need to supply any additional multilingual systems on the embedded system.

The experiments will show that it was possible to find such algorithms. Due to the achieved speed (only fractions of a second per language) these algorithms are called on-the-fly generation of multilingual acoustic models (otfMHMM). The major benefit of these algorithms is that there is no longer an exponential dependency on the number of languages the speech dialog system has to support, as only the actually needed system is generated on the embedded system.

Figure 4.4 depicts how such a process could look like for two possible applications of the work in this thesis, multilingual destination input and music selection. In the

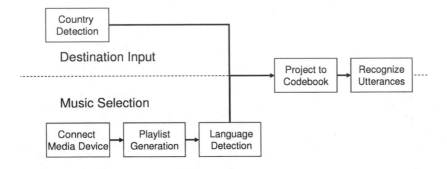

Figure 4.4: Fast generation of multilingual HMMs depending on the current task

destination selection, the system determines the language of nearby destinations. In the music selection, the languages of interest can be determined from the language distribution in the music database. There are two tasks that are common to both examples, language identification and the generation of HMMs that fit to the codebook of the current main language. When all the tasks run on embedded systems, no additional systems need to be provided and the required multilingual phoneme models can be generated online.

In this thesis no details about language identification are provided as it is widely used and there are freely available tools like TextCat [Noor 09] for 69 different languages. Language recognition rates are in the range of 90% or higher for 30 letter sequences [Ueda 90].

The ideas of this section were published in [Raab 09a, Raab 09c].

4.4.2   Optimal Projections

In the literature many distances between Gaussian Mixture Models have been proposed. Examples are an approximated Kullback Leibler divergence [Hers 07], the likelihood difference on a development set [Juan 85, Koeh 01] or the L2 distance [Jian 05, Jens 07]. The likelihood difference on a development set has the disadvantage that development data is necessary. This thesis applied the L2 distance between Gaussians, as a closed solution exists for this distance, which is not the case for the Kullback-Leibler distance.

The L2 distance between two Gaussian mixture models A and B defined by

$$D_{L2}(A, B) = \int (\boldsymbol{\alpha}^T \mathbf{a}(\mathbf{x}) - \boldsymbol{\beta}^T \mathbf{b}(\mathbf{x}))^2 dx \qquad (4.8)$$

$\boldsymbol{\alpha}$ and $\boldsymbol{\beta}$ are the weight vectors of the Gaussian vectors $\mathbf{a}$ and $\mathbf{b}$.

$$\boldsymbol{\alpha} = \begin{pmatrix} w_1^a \\ w_2^a \\ \vdots \\ w_n^a \end{pmatrix}, \; \mathbf{a}(\mathbf{x}) = \begin{pmatrix} \mathcal{N}(\mathbf{x}; \boldsymbol{\mu}_1^a, \boldsymbol{\Sigma}_1^a) \\ \mathcal{N}(\mathbf{x}; \boldsymbol{\mu}_2^a, \boldsymbol{\Sigma}_2^a) \\ \vdots \\ \mathcal{N}(\mathbf{x}; \boldsymbol{\mu}_n^a \boldsymbol{\Sigma}_n^a) \end{pmatrix} \qquad (4.9)$$

$$\boldsymbol{\beta} = \begin{pmatrix} w_1^b \\ w_2^b \\ \vdots \\ w_m^b \end{pmatrix}, \; \mathbf{b}(\mathbf{x}) = \begin{pmatrix} \mathcal{N}(\mathbf{x}; \boldsymbol{\mu}_1^b, \boldsymbol{\Sigma}_1^b) \\ \mathcal{N}(\mathbf{x}; \boldsymbol{\mu}_2^b, \boldsymbol{\Sigma}_2^b) \\ \vdots \\ \mathcal{N}(\mathbf{x}; \boldsymbol{\mu}_m^b, \boldsymbol{\Sigma}_m^b) \end{pmatrix} \qquad (4.10)$$

The distance D_{L2} can be calculated as follows

$$\begin{aligned} D_{L2}(A, B) &= \int (\boldsymbol{\alpha}^T \mathbf{a}(\mathbf{x}) - \boldsymbol{\beta}^T \mathbf{b}(\mathbf{x}))^2 \, dx \\ &= \int [(\boldsymbol{\alpha}^T \mathbf{a}(\mathbf{x}))^2 - 2\boldsymbol{\alpha}^T \mathbf{a}(\mathbf{x})\boldsymbol{\beta}^T \mathbf{b}(\mathbf{x}) + (\boldsymbol{\beta}^T \mathbf{b}(\mathbf{x}))^2] \, dx \\ &= \sum_i \sum_j \alpha_i \alpha_j \int a_i(\mathbf{x}) a_j(\mathbf{x}) \, dx \\ &\quad - 2 \sum_i \sum_j \alpha_i \beta_j \int a_i(\mathbf{x}) b_j(\mathbf{x}) \, dx \\ &\quad + \sum_i \sum_j \beta_i \beta_j \int b_i(\mathbf{x}) b_j(\mathbf{x}) \, dx \end{aligned} \qquad (4.11)$$

with $a_i(\mathbf{x}) = \mathcal{N}(\mathbf{x}; \boldsymbol{\mu}_i^a, \boldsymbol{\Sigma}_i^a)$ and $b_i(\mathbf{x}) = \mathcal{N}(\mathbf{x}; \boldsymbol{\mu}_i^b, \boldsymbol{\Sigma}_i^b)$. In order to solve this problem, the correlation $\int \mathcal{N}(\mathbf{x}; \boldsymbol{\mu}_1, \boldsymbol{\Sigma}_1) \mathcal{N}(\mathbf{x}; \boldsymbol{\mu}_2, \boldsymbol{\Sigma}_2) \, dx$ between the Gaussians needs to be calculated. [Pete 08] state that

$$\mathcal{N}(\mathbf{x}; \boldsymbol{\mu}_1, \boldsymbol{\Sigma}_1)\mathcal{N}(\mathbf{x}; \boldsymbol{\mu}_2, \boldsymbol{\Sigma}_2) = c_c \mathcal{N}(\mathbf{x}; \boldsymbol{\mu}_c, \boldsymbol{\Sigma}_c) \qquad (4.12)$$

where $\boldsymbol{\mu}$ and $\boldsymbol{\Sigma}$ are the mean and the covariances of the Gaussians. The elements of the resulting Gaussian $c_c \mathcal{N}(\mathbf{x}; \boldsymbol{\mu}_c, \boldsymbol{\Sigma}_c)$ are

$$c_c = \mathcal{N}(\boldsymbol{\mu}_1; \boldsymbol{\mu}_2, (\boldsymbol{\Sigma}_1 + \boldsymbol{\Sigma}2))$$

$$= \frac{1}{\sqrt{det(2\pi(\Sigma_1 + \Sigma_2))}} e^{\left[-1/2(\mu_1-\mu_2)^T(\Sigma_1+\Sigma_2)^{-1}(\mu_1-\mu_2)\right]} \tag{4.13}$$

$$\mu_c = (\Sigma_1^{-1} + \Sigma_2^{-1})^{-1}(\Sigma_1^{-1}\mu_1 + \Sigma_2^{-1}\mu_2) \tag{4.14}$$

$$\Sigma_c = (\Sigma_1^{-1} + \Sigma_2^{-1})^{-1} \tag{4.15}$$

Thus

$$\int \mathcal{N}(\mathbf{x}; \mu_1, \Sigma_1)\mathcal{N}(\mathbf{x}; \mu_2, \Sigma_2)\, d\mathbf{x}$$

$$= \int c_c \mathcal{N}(\mathbf{x}; \mu_c, \Sigma_c) d\mathbf{x}$$

$$= c_c \underbrace{\int \mathcal{N}(\mathbf{x}; \mu_c, \Sigma_c) d\mathbf{x}}_{=1}$$

$$= c_c \tag{4.16}$$

With this, all correlations between all Gaussians can be calculated and written in three matrices $\mathbf{M}^{AA}$, $\mathbf{M}^{AB}$ and $\mathbf{M}^{BB}$.

$$M_{ij}^{AA} = \int a_i(\mathbf{x})a_j(\mathbf{x})d\mathbf{x} \tag{4.17}$$

$$M_{ij}^{AB} = \int a_i(\mathbf{x})b_j(\mathbf{x})d\mathbf{x} \tag{4.18}$$

$$M_{ij}^{BB} = \int b_i(\mathbf{x})b_j(\mathbf{x})d\mathbf{x} \tag{4.19}$$

Hence Equation (4.11) can be written as

$$D_{L2}(A, B) = \sum_i \sum_j \alpha_i\alpha_j M_{ij}^{AA} - 2\sum_i \sum_j \alpha_i\beta_j M_{ij}^{AB} + \sum_i \sum_j \beta_i\beta_j M_{ij}^{BB}$$

$$= \alpha^T \mathbf{M}^{AA}\alpha - 2\alpha^T \mathbf{M}^{AB}\beta + \beta^T \mathbf{M}^{BB}\beta \tag{4.20}$$

The purpose of Equation (4.20) is to measure distances between different *given* Gaussian mixtures. This is straightforward as long as α and β are known, which is the regular case. However, for this work it is more interesting to find an α_{min} that minimizes $D_{L2}(A, B)$. The solutions from this section were first presented in [Raab 09c].

This α_{min} models the Gaussian mixture distribution B as well as possible when only Gaussians from A are available. Thus the α that minimizes this distance is searched. The derivative of D_{L2} with respect to α is:

$$\frac{\partial D_{L2}}{\partial \alpha} = 2\,\mathrm{M}^{AA}\alpha - 2\,\mathrm{M}^{AB}\beta \qquad (4.21)$$

In order to find the minimum the gradient is set to $\vec{0} = (0, 0, \ldots, 0)^T$.

$$2\,\mathrm{M}^{AA}\alpha_{min} - 2\,\mathrm{M}^{AB}\beta = \vec{0} \qquad (4.22)$$

Solving this equation leads to the optimal weights α_{min}.

$$\alpha_{min} = (\mathrm{M}^{AA})^{-1}\mathrm{M}^{AB}\beta \qquad (4.23)$$

This α_{min} is a true minimum when the second derivative of D_{L2} is positive definite. The second derivative is $2\,M^{AA}$. M^{AA} is a correlation matrix, and therefore positive semidefinite. As long as none of the Gaussians is linear dependent on the other Gaussians, this matrix is positive definite and therefore α_{min} a true minimum. This α_{min} is therefore the first proposed projection.

Definition 4.4.1 (Projection 1):

An optimal projection from GMM B to A that minimizes the D_{L2} error $D_{L2}(A, B)$.

$$\alpha_{min} = (\mathrm{M}^{AA})^{-1}\mathrm{M}^{AB}\beta$$

The projection creates negative weights for Gaussians, and there is no normalization of the sum of the Gaussian weights.

Despite the fact that the proposed projection is optimal with regard to the L2 distance, it is likely to be suboptimal for the use in a common speech recognizer. The reasons are that

1. The elements of α_{min} do not sum to one, thus some states can always have higher scores than others.

2. There are negative weights for Gaussians. In our decoder these values have been replaced by a log likelihood threshold.

The first problem can be solved with the Lagrange constraint that all weights have to sum to one. The Lagrange function to minimize can be stated as:

$$L(\boldsymbol{\alpha}, \lambda) = \boldsymbol{\alpha}^T \mathbf{M}^{AA} \boldsymbol{\alpha} - 2\boldsymbol{\alpha}^T \mathbf{M}^{AB} \boldsymbol{\beta} + \boldsymbol{\beta}^T \mathbf{M}^{BB} \boldsymbol{\beta} + \lambda(\sum_i (\alpha_i) - 1) \qquad (4.24)$$

with the additional Lagrange multiplier λ. Differentiating this function gives

$$\frac{\partial L}{\partial \boldsymbol{\alpha}} = 2 \, \mathbf{M}^{AA} \boldsymbol{\alpha} - 2 \, \mathbf{M}^{AB} \boldsymbol{\beta} + \begin{pmatrix} \lambda \\ \vdots \\ \lambda \end{pmatrix} \qquad (4.25)$$

$$\frac{\partial L}{\partial \lambda} = \sum_i (\alpha_i) - 1 \qquad (4.26)$$

The following gives one representation that shows both derivations in closed form

$$\frac{\partial L}{\partial (\boldsymbol{\alpha}, \lambda)} = \begin{pmatrix} 2 \, \mathbf{M}^{AA} & \vec{\mathbf{1}} \\ \vec{\mathbf{1}}^T & 0 \end{pmatrix} \begin{pmatrix} \boldsymbol{\alpha} \\ \lambda \end{pmatrix} - \begin{pmatrix} 2 \, \mathbf{M}^{AB} & \vec{\mathbf{0}} \\ \vec{\mathbf{0}}^T & 1/\lambda \end{pmatrix} \begin{pmatrix} \boldsymbol{\beta} \\ \lambda \end{pmatrix} \qquad (4.27)$$

with $\vec{\mathbf{1}} = (1, 1, \ldots, 1)^T$.

Setting the derivation to $\vec{\mathbf{0}}$ and removing λ from the second matrix leads to the second projection.

Definition 4.4.2 (Projection 2):

An optimal projection from GMM B to A that minimizes the D_{L2} error $D_{L2}(A, B)$.

$$\begin{pmatrix} \boldsymbol{\alpha}_{min} \\ \lambda \end{pmatrix} = \begin{pmatrix} 2 \, \mathbf{M}^{AA} & \vec{\mathbf{1}} \\ \vec{\mathbf{1}}^T & 0 \end{pmatrix}^{-1} \cdot \begin{pmatrix} 2 \, \mathbf{M}^{AB} & \vec{\mathbf{0}} \\ \vec{\mathbf{0}}^T & 1 \end{pmatrix} \begin{pmatrix} \boldsymbol{\beta} \\ 1 \end{pmatrix}$$

The constraint that all Gaussian weights have to sum to one is enforced. There can be negative weights for Gaussians after the projection.

The issue of negative weights is a more difficult convex optimization problem [Boyd 04]. A common method to solve it are the Karush Khun Tucker constraints [Kuhn 51]. These are basically a generalization of the Lagrange constraints and can work with inequalities through slack variables s that transform every inequality in an equality, which can be solved as any Lagrange constraint. In the case here, an inequality constraint has to be introduced for every element of $\boldsymbol{\alpha}$. This gives the new function KKT for the distance between the mixture distribution A and B.

$$KKT(\boldsymbol{\alpha}, \lambda, \boldsymbol{\gamma}) = \boldsymbol{\alpha}^T \mathbf{M}^{AA} \boldsymbol{\alpha} - 2\boldsymbol{\alpha}^T \mathbf{M}^{AB} \boldsymbol{\beta} + \boldsymbol{\beta}^T \mathbf{M}^{BB} \boldsymbol{\beta}$$

$$+ \lambda(\sum_i (\alpha_i) - 1) + \sum_{i=1}^{n} \gamma_i(-\alpha_i + s_i^2) \tag{4.28}$$

with $\boldsymbol{\gamma} = (\gamma_1, \gamma_2, \ldots, \gamma_n)$ and $\mathbf{s} = (s_1, s_2, \ldots, s_n)$.

The KKT function has always to give the same result as D_{L2}. This means either γ_i is zero, or $\alpha_i + s_i^2$ is zero. When α_i is zero, constraint i is said to be active, otherwise the constraint is inactive. If constraint i is active, γ_i is greater 0. To find the optimal solution, all possible combinations of active constraints and inactive constraints need to be evaluated, and one of these solutions will be the optimal solution that fits the constraints.

In practice it is not possible to check all the possible combinations for the optimal value. Similar problems have to be solved for Neural Networks [Plat 88, Bieh 90]. Basically, the idea is to perform a gradient descent on the optimization criterion and a gradient ascent on the equality constraint. [Bieh 90] show that a quadratic optimization problem that ignores negative values converges with gradient descent. The actual implementation was sensitive to a good setting of update weights, as both equality and inequality constraints had to be considered. Nevertheless, the sequential iterative optimization algorithm achieved on average almost the same L2 distance as Projection 1 with only three iterations. This gradient descent is the third proposed projection.

Definition 4.4.3 (Projection 3):

An "almost optimal" projection from GMM B to A that minimizes the D_{L2} error $D_{L2}(A, B)$. The weights are determined in a gradient search that descents on the distance criterion. They sum to one and are not negative.

When these projections are applied to the HBAS recognizers not all Gaussians are comparable, as the different languages have different LDAs (Linear Discriminant Analyses). Therefore each Gaussian was saved before it was modified by an LDA. These Gaussians are also used for the approximated projections in the next section.

4.4.3   Approximated Projections

In the previous section, three different projections with different constraints were introduced. Each of them has some disadvantages for employment in an embedded speech recognition system. The first two projections, as they did not produce correct probability distributions, and the last one, as correct distributions can only be found with a gradient descent. Therefore, this section proposes some experimentally motivated projections.

The goal of each projection is to map all HMMs of all L languages to one fixed set of N Gaussians (= Recognition Codebook, RC) which can be either mono- or multilingual. Such a mapping can be achieved by mapping all M^l Gaussians of each additional language codebook (= Monolingual Codebook, MC^l) to the RC. Each Gaussian $\mathcal{N}$ is represented by its mean $\boldsymbol{\mu}$ and covariance matrix $\boldsymbol{\Sigma}$. The Mahalanobis distance measures the distance between Gaussians (D_G). Only the covariances of the Gaussians to replace are considered to avoid influences of flat (=with large variance) Gaussians in the RC.

Definition 4.4.4 (Projection 4):

An approximated projection that only compares individual Gaussians in the different codebooks to derive a mapping. Each additional language Gaussian is replaced by another Gaussian according to map_G.

$$map_G(\mathcal{N}^i_{MC^l}) = \mathcal{N}^j_{RC}, \ 0 \le i < M^l, 0 \le j < N, 0 \le l < L$$
$$j = \arg\min_k D_G(\boldsymbol{\mu}^i_{MC^l}, \boldsymbol{\mu}^k_{RC}, \boldsymbol{\Sigma}^i_{MC^l}) \qquad (4.29)$$

When all Gaussians from the main language are in the RC, there are further possibilities how HMMs from other languages can be linked to the RC. All states from the main language map only to Gaussians from the RC. Thus when all S states are mapped to RS main language states only Gaussians from the RC are used. The same is true when all HMMs H are mapped to main language HMMs RH. Both of these additional mappings have the advantage that they consider the combination of Gaussians in their distance.

We map states based on the minimum Mahalanobis distance (D_S) between the expected values of their probability distributions. In the system of this thesis the probability distribution $p_\mathbf{s}$ of every state $\mathbf{s}$ is a Gaussian mixture distribution with M^l Gaussians.

$$p_{\mathbf{s}_l}(\mathbf{x}) = \sum_{i=0}^{M^l} w_i \mathcal{N}(\mathbf{x}; \boldsymbol{\mu}_i, \boldsymbol{\Sigma}_i) \tag{4.30}$$

The expected value of $\mathbf{x}$ for each state $\mathbf{s}$ is then

$$
\begin{aligned}
E(p_{\mathbf{s}_l}(\mathbf{x})) &= E\Big(\sum_{i=1}^{M^l} w_{\mathbf{s}_l}^i \mathcal{N}(\mathbf{x}; \boldsymbol{\mu}_i, \boldsymbol{\Sigma}_i)\Big) \\
&= \sum_{i=1}^{M^l} E(w_{\mathbf{s}_l}^i \mathcal{N}(\mathbf{x}; \boldsymbol{\mu}_i, \boldsymbol{\Sigma}_i)) \\
&= \sum_{i=1}^{M^l} w_{\mathbf{s}_l}^i \boldsymbol{\mu}_i
\end{aligned}
\tag{4.31}
$$

The covariance which is needed for the Mahalanobis distance is a global diagonal covariance $\boldsymbol{\Sigma}_{All}$ estimated on all training samples. With D_S a state based mapping is defined as

---

Definition 4.4.5 (Projection 5):

An approximated projection that compares states from additional languages to main language HMM states to derive a mapping. Each individual HMM state is replaced by another HMM state according to map_S.

$$\mathbf{map_S}(\mathbf{s}_l^i) = \mathbf{s}_{RS}^j, 0 \le i < S_l, 0 \le j < RS, 0 \le l < L$$
$$j = \arg\min_k D_S(E(\mathbf{s}_l^i), E(\mathbf{s}_{RS}^k), \boldsymbol{\Sigma}_{All}) \tag{4.32}$$

Based on D_S a distance between HMMs (D_H) can be defined. When each phoneme is modeled by a three state HMM the distance between two phonemes $\mathbf{q}_1$ and $\mathbf{q}_2$ is

$$D_H(\mathbf{q}_1, \mathbf{q}_2) = \sum_{i=1}^{3} D_S(\mathbf{s}_{\mathbf{q}_1}^i, \mathbf{s}_{\mathbf{q}_2}^i) \tag{4.33}$$

Definition 4.4.6 (Projection 6):

An approximated projection that compares HMMs from additional languages to main language HMMs to derive a mapping. Each additional language HMM is replaced by a main language HMM according to map_H.

$$\mathbf{map_H}(\mathbf{q}_l^i) = \mathbf{q}_{RH}^j, 0 \le i < H_l, 0 \le j < RH, 0 \le l < L$$
$$j = \arg\min_k D_H(\mathbf{q}_l^i, \mathbf{q}_{RH}^k) \tag{4.34}$$

D_G and D_S provide consistently good performance for different tests, while they use rather different information for their calculation. Therefore this thesis also tests a combined map_{G+S}.

Definition 4.4.7 (Projection 7):

An approximated projection that compares both Gaussians and HMM states to derive a mapping. Each additional language state gets a new output distribution probability according to map_{G+S}.

$$\mathbf{map_{G+S}}(\mathbf{s}_l^i) =$$

$$\gamma_{G+S}\,\mathbf{map_S}(\mathbf{s}_l^i) + (1 - \gamma_{G+S})\begin{pmatrix} w_{\mathbf{s}_l^i}^1 map_G(\mathcal{N}_{MC^l}^1) \\ w_{\mathbf{s}_l^i}^2 map_G(\mathcal{N}_{MC^l}^2) \\ \vdots \\ w_{\mathbf{s}_l^i}^{M^l} map_G(\mathcal{N}_{MC^l}^{M^l}) \end{pmatrix}$$

$$0 \le l < L, 0 \le i < S_l \tag{4.35}$$

with the combination weight γ_{G+S}.

γ_{G+S} has to be determined in experiments. An additional retraining after each of the projections would probably increase the performance. In the experiments no retraining was performed, as this keeps the creation of new multilingual systems as simple as possible and on-demand acoustic model creation feasible.

4.4.4 Overview of Projections

In the previous two sections, several methods for the projection of HMMs from one language to another were proposed. Table 4.1 summarizes the main information about them. The method column describes which information is used for the projection. The probability column indicates, if the result of the projection is a correct probability distribution.

Projection	Method	Probability
Pro1	L2 minimization	no
Pro2	L2 minimization	no
Pro3	L2 minimization	yes
Pro4	Gaussian mapping	yes
Pro5	State mapping	yes
Pro6	HMM mapping	yes
Pro7	Pro4 + Pro5	yes

Table 4.1: Comparison of projection methods.

4.5 Scalable Architecture

The MWC algorithm (Section 4.3) allows to improve the baseline systems with a limited number of additional parameters. However, this algorithm increases the training effort exponentially, as theoretically MWCs for all language combinations have to be built. The otfMHMM algorithm (Section 4.4) allows to generate multilingual models from monolingual models much faster than traditional algorithms. However, this speed up comes at the cost of reduced performance.

A combination of the two algorithms thus leads to a scalable architecture that can provide new systems rapidly for all language combinations and at the same time allows to increase the performance by allowing more additional Gaussians in the MWC step. The idea of the scalable architecture was presented in [Raab 09b].

Figure 4.5 shows how the process introduced in Figure 4.4 can be modified to integrate the MWC algorithm. This time, there are three tasks that are common to both examples, language identification, MWC based codebook creation and the generation of HMMs on top of the generated codebook. When all the tasks run on embedded systems, no additional acoustic models need to be provided and the required multilingual phoneme models can be generated online. The other components like language detection were discussed in Section 4.4.

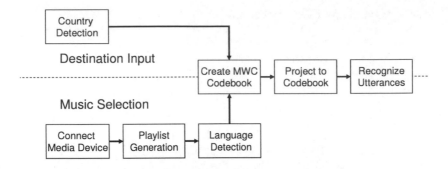

Figure 4.5: Generating a user adapted system on an embedded system.

Classifier	US_City
GE_1024 C1	65.6
IT_1024 C1	62.8
SP_1024 C1	56.1
FR_1024 C1	64.2
US_1024 C1	75.5

Table 4.2: Native language codebooks from several languages on an English test set.

4.6   Adaptation

4.6.1   Accent Detection and Language Identification through Codebook Share Rates

This section presents one of the simpler algorithms. The improvements of multilingual classifiers with multilingual codebooks show that codebooks differ between languages. Table 4.2 gives some example results of classifiers built on codebooks that were trained on five different languages. The actual training of the HMMs was always performed with the same set of English data. As expected, the English codebook has the best performance. More interesting here are the big differences between the codebooks.

From this set of results, one can conclude that codebooks for different languages differ significantly, and each codebook has to capture some aspects which characterize this language. Thus, it can be assumed that the codebook of the spoken language has better fitting Gaussians than the codebooks from other languages when codebooks from several languages compete against each other.

The standard Gaussian likelihood is used for the evaluation if a Gaussian fits better than other Gaussians. Thus, in this first scenario the author believes that codebooks can be used for language identification of native speech.

In car infotainment systems, however, another scenario might be more frequent. Determining the users main language can easily be done by selecting the language the user sets for the haptic interface. In the multilingual scenario, as introduced already a couple of times the user might now utter foreign music titles or travel destinations. In this case, the assumption is that both the native codebook and the codebook of the spoken language have in average better fitting Gaussians. As the native language is known from the user interface language, the other fitting codebook must be the codebook of the spoken language.

Therefore, in this second case, the native language of the speaker and the spoken language would be determined. This offers the chance to deliberately adapt to that special accent.

4.6.2   Durational Modeling

[Tomo 01a] showed in her analysis of Japanese and Chinese accented speech that non-native speakers have slightly longer phoneme durations than native speakers. Therefore HMMs should better model non-native speech if the self-loop probabilities of the HMM states are increased.

A pseudo code version of the code is given below.

$$numStates = numberOfStates$$
$$changeFactor = x$$
$$\textbf{for } i = 1 \text{ to numStates } \textbf{do}$$
$$\quad change = i.selfLoop * changeFactor$$
$$\quad \textbf{if } i.selfLoop + change < 0.99 \textbf{ then}$$
$$\quad\quad i.selfLoop = i.selfLoop + change$$
$$\quad\quad i.trans = i.selfLoop - change$$
$$\quad \textbf{else}$$
$$\quad\quad i.selfLoop = 0.99$$
$$\quad\quad i.trans = 0.01$$
$$\quad \textbf{end if}$$
$$\textbf{end for}$$

The change factor is set to different values in the experiments. The code example shows the simplicity of this approach, but due to the theoretic motivation it is tested in the experimental section.

4.6.3   Frequency Band Weight Adaptation

[Arsl 96] showed that mid-range frequencies (1KHz-2.5 kHz) are more important for accent detection than the frequencies below one kilohertz. He argues that this is due to two reasons. First, small tongue movements already cause severe changes in higher frequencies, which is not this pronounced for lower frequencies. Second, people hear better at low frequencies and know that low frequencies are more important to produce understandable utterances in the foreign language. Therefore they first aim to copy the low frequency behavior of the foreign language.

However, the aim here is to improve speech recognition performance for non-native speech. As stated above, non-native speech differs more severely for higher frequencies. The conclusion is that it should be possible to improve speech recognition performance for non-native speech by increasing the weight on lower frequencies. This can be done with a change of the range of the typical triangles filters used for MFCCs. Another possibility is to change the covariance matrix of the Gaussians, so that errors in higher frequencies have less impact on the likelihood that a feature vector was generated by this Gaussian. Yet, the HMMs of a speech recognizer work on a signal that was already transformed by a couple of different transformations. After all the transformations it is no longer straightforward to decide how a Gaussian has to be changed to treat different speech frequencies differently.

If the second approach can be realized, it has the additional advantage that an existing recognizer can be modified for the improved recognition of non-native speech, and at the same time, the modification can be undone for the recognition of native speech. A modification of the MEL filter-bank requires a retraining, and will almost certainly lead to an irreversible performance loss on native speech. Therefore the author chose to implement the second approach.

Modification of a Gaussian

The first question to answer is how a multivariate Gaussian has to be modified to weight some dimensions higher than others for its likelihood output. For this general aspect, it is irrelevant what the single dimensions of the Gaussian mean. This will be discussed in the next part.

A multivariate Gaussian A in a n-dimensional feature space is defined as

$$A(\mathbf{x}) = \frac{1}{(2\pi)^{n/2} \left|\mathbf{\Sigma}\right|^{1/2}} \, e^{-1/2(\mathbf{x}-\boldsymbol{\mu})^T \mathbf{\Sigma}^{-1}(\mathbf{x}-\boldsymbol{\mu})}$$

with the covariance matrix Σ being

$$\Sigma = \begin{pmatrix} v_{11} & v_{12} & \cdots & v_{1n} \\ v_{21} & v_{22} & \cdots & v_{2n} \\ \vdots & \ddots & \ddots & \vdots \\ v_{n1} & v_{n2} & \cdots & v_{nn} \end{pmatrix}$$

It can be seen, that the term in front of the Euler constant is independent of the feature vector $\mathbf{x}$. Thus it can be ignored for modifications of the likelihood function of the Gaussian such that differences in some dimensions affect the likelihood of the Gaussians more and other dimensions affect the likelihood less. Consequently, only the exponent has to be considered, which is the Mahalanobis distance. The smaller the Mahalanobis distance between the feature vector and the mean vector is, the higher the likelihood of the Gaussian. Differences in one dimension will have less impact on the n-dimensional Mahalanobis distance when the variance of the Gaussian is high in this dimension. Thus, if the variance in one dimension i is modified with a factor $(g_i)^2$, the likelihood calculation can be changed as desired.

If the variance of each dimension is multiplied with a factor $(g_i)^2$, the covariances v_{ij} are also affected. The new covariances $\overline{v_{ij}}$ are

$$\overline{v_{ij}} = \sqrt{\overline{v_{ii}}} * \sqrt{\overline{v_{jj}}} = \sqrt{g_i^2 v_{ii}} * \sqrt{g_j^2 v_{jj}} = g_i g_j * \sqrt{v_{ii} v_{jj}} = g_i g_j v_{ij}$$

This leads to the new covariance matrix $\overline{\Sigma}$

$$\overline{\Sigma} = \begin{pmatrix} g_1^2 v_{11} & g_1 g_2 v_{12} & \cdots & g_1 g_n v_{1n} \\ g_2 g_1 v_{21} & g_2^2 v_{22} & \cdots & g_2 g_n v_{2n} \\ \vdots & \ddots & \ddots & \vdots \\ g_n g_1 v_{n1} & g_n g_2 v_{n2} & \cdots & g_n^2 v_{nn} \end{pmatrix}$$

which is the same as Σ multiplied with $\mathbf{G} * \Sigma * \mathbf{G}^T$ where $\mathbf{G}$ is defined as

$$\mathbf{G} = \begin{pmatrix} g_1 & 0 & \cdots & 0 \\ 0 & g_2 & \cdots & 0 \\ \vdots & \ddots & \ddots & \vdots \\ 0 & 0 & \cdots & g_n \end{pmatrix}$$

When the correct Gaussians are transformed, each g reduces or increases the influence of one frequency band. Therefore this algorithm is called Frequency Band Weight Adaptation (FBWA).

Which Gaussian to transform?

This question might at first seem misplaced, as it is clear that the goal is to modify
the Gaussians of the codebook. However, the codebook Gaussians are not based on
the log-mel frequency representation of the speech signal. To summarize, an LDA and
the Discrete Cosine Transform (DCT) are applied to the frequency representation of
the speech signal before the Gaussians are estimated. Thus the dimensions on which
the codebook Gaussians are based are not directly related to different frequencies in
the speech signal. Therefore the Gaussians that are defined in the Cepstrum have to
be transformed to Gaussians in the spectrum to allow the desired modifications.

Both the LDA and the discrete cosine transform are matrix multiplications and
thus linear transformations. A Gaussian remains a Gaussian under linear transformations. More specifically, a Gaussian A as defined above becomes the Gaussian B
under the linear transformation matrix $\mathbf{T}$. The new Gaussian B has the mean $\boldsymbol{\mu}_B$

$$\boldsymbol{\mu}_B = \mathbf{T}\boldsymbol{\mu}_A$$

and the covariance matrix $\boldsymbol{\Sigma}_B$.

$$\boldsymbol{\Sigma}_B = \mathbf{T} * \boldsymbol{\Sigma}_A * \mathbf{T}^T$$

This can be applied for the LDA with the LDA matrix $\mathbf{L}$ and the discrete cosine
transform with transformation matrix $\mathbf{C}$. Thus a Gaussian of the codebook (in the
LDA space) can be transformed to a Gaussian in the MEL frequency space (more
exactly, the log MEL frequency space). In this space, each dimension can be aligned
to a frequency range (see Appendix C).

$$\boldsymbol{\Sigma}_{MEL} = \mathbf{C}^{-1} * \mathbf{L}^{-1} * \boldsymbol{\Sigma}_{LDA} * \mathbf{L}^{-1^T} * \mathbf{C}^{-1^T}$$

In practice, the $\boldsymbol{\Sigma}_{MEL}$ matrix will not be exactly the same as if it had been estimated
directly from the log-mel feature vectors, as typically the LDA and the DCT are used
to reduce the dimension of the feature space. The intension of this is to get a lower
dimensional feature space that still contains the relevant information. In the rest
of this section this effect is ignored for simplicity. However, this aspect has to be
considered in an implementation. The correct treatment of dimensionality reduction
is described in Section 4.6.3.

It is clear that the mean vectors of all Gaussians remain constant in all feature
spaces when only the variance of the Gaussians is changed. The Gaussian with the
covariance matrix $\boldsymbol{\Sigma}_{MEL}$ is a Gaussian in the MEL feature space. Its dimensions

correspond to frequency bands of the speech signal. Hence this Gaussian can be multiplied with the **G** matrix as defined above, to weight different frequencies differently. This leads to

$$\overline{\Sigma_{MEL}} = \mathbf{G} * \mathbf{C}^{-1} * \mathbf{L}^{-1} * \Sigma_{LDA} * \mathbf{L}^{-1^T} * \mathbf{C}^{-1^T} * \mathbf{G}^T$$

Finally the modified Gaussian in the MEL space has to be transformed back in the LDA space to be applied during the speech recognition process, leading to

$$\overline{\Sigma_{LDA}} = \mathbf{L} * \mathbf{C} * \mathbf{G} * \mathbf{C}^{-1} * \mathbf{L}^{-1} * \Sigma_{LDA} * \mathbf{L}^{-1^T} * \mathbf{C}^{-1^T} * \mathbf{G}^T * \mathbf{C}^T * \mathbf{L}^T$$

The used cosine transform is orthogonal, thus the $\mathbf{C}^{-1^T} = \mathbf{C}$, and the formula reduces to

$$\overline{\Sigma_{LDA}} = \mathbf{L} * \mathbf{C} * \mathbf{G} * \mathbf{C}^{-1} * \mathbf{L}^{-1} * \Sigma_{LDA} * \mathbf{L}^{-1^T} * \mathbf{C} * \mathbf{G}^T * \mathbf{C}^{-1} * \mathbf{L}^T \qquad (4.36)$$

One final statement concerns technical aspects. The LDA in the HBAS recognizer transforms not only the feature space, but also discards some of the less relevant dimensions. But in most cases, the codebook with Gaussians before the LDA is still available. In these cases, it will be better to use the codebook before the LDA modification as starting point, and perform the following operations

$$\overline{\Sigma_{LDA}} = \mathbf{L} * \mathbf{C} * \mathbf{G} * \mathbf{C}^{-1} * \Sigma_{DCT} * \mathbf{C} * \mathbf{G}^T * \mathbf{C}^{-1} * \mathbf{L}^T \qquad (4.37)$$

Both Equation (4.36) and (4.37) generate new Gaussians optimized for the recognition of non-native speech.

Retraining or Not?

No matter if Equation (4.36) or (4.37) is applied, it still is arguable if the same HMMs as before can be used after the Gaussians have been changed. It is certainly true, a training **after** the Gaussians have been modified will lead to different HMMs. First of all, the LDA matrix itself will change, and second the alignment during the Baum-Welch algorithm will change.

Yet, the author believes that not performing a retraining is the correct way, as the Gaussians, the alignment and the LDA matrix itself are all optimized for the training data. Modifying the Gaussians and performing a retraining on **native** speech will hardly give improved performance. The whole motivation why the Gaussians are

Feature Space	Dimension
MEL	162
Log-MEL	162
CEP	99
LDA	32

Table 4.3: Example dimensions of feature space. The dimensions originate from 18 Mel filterbands and the concatenation of 9 frames.

modified is to account for a mismatch of the native training data to the non-native test, for which no matching training data is available.

Correct Treatment of Dimension Reduction

In the previous section, the fact of dimensionality reduction was ignored, thus making the assumption that all matrices are square and have the same dimension. This simplification allowed for example to write

$$\Sigma_{MEL} = \mathbf{C}^{-1} * \mathbf{L}^{-1} * \Sigma_{LDA} * \mathbf{L}^{-1^T} * \mathbf{C}^{-1^T} \tag{4.38}$$

without worrying about matrix dimensions. In the HBAS system however, both the DCT and the LDA are used for dimensionality reduction. A set of common dimensions of the feature spaces is shown in Table 4.3. The dimensions originate from the number of Mel filters (18, see Section 2.1) and the concatenation of several frames (in this example 9, see Section 4.1). This leads to the fact that Equation (4.38) actually looks like Equation (4.39), where the regarding matrix dimensions are indicated in parentheses after the matrix. The matrix operations like transpose and invert are always executed on the square version of the matrix, however, for the multiplication only parts of the matrices have to be used.

$$\Sigma_{MEL,(162x162)} = \mathbf{C}^{-1}_{(162x99)} * \mathbf{L}^{-1}_{(99x32)} * \Sigma_{LDA,(32x32)} * \mathbf{L}^{-1^T}_{(32x99)} * \mathbf{C}^{-1^T}_{(99x162)} \tag{4.39}$$

Similarly, all Equations from Section 4.6.3 have to be modified for correct transformations.

4.6.4 Model Merging

Model Merging was originally proposed by [Witt 99b, Witt 99a] for continuous HMM systems. The idea is to combine models of the source and target language of the speaker to derive models that match the non-native pronunciation of the speaker. In the original work, experiments with and without non-native adaptation data were performed. In the first case an improvement of 41% relative WER was achieved, in the second case still 27% relative WER were achieved. As this thesis tries to avoid the use of non-native adaptation data, only the second case is considered. In this case, the algorithm works as follows:

- Define a mapping between source and target language models

- Each state is replaced by $\alpha\, State_{source} + (1 - \alpha)\, State_{target}$

where α is a weight between zero and one.

In the original work the mapping was derived by comparing phoneme recognition results of accented speech. This means that the accented speech was first recognized with a recognizer of the source language and a second time with a recognizer of the target language. The confusions that occurred were manually checked, and the accepted most likely confusions defined the mapping. Such a mapping requires therefore both accented training data and human work.

In the context of this thesis, it was more desirable to reduce the complexity to derive such a mapping. Therefore different fully automatic mappings were tested. The first one was the distance between the expected values of states, as it was used before for Projection 5 in Section 4.4.3. The second tested distance was the HMM based distance for Projection 6. To distinguish these two distances, the distance that only merges states is called State Merging and the second distance is called Model Merging.

A second issue when transferring the original idea to the work in this thesis is that the number of Gaussians in each state were doubled for each HMM state. This is no problem in a continuous HMM system, but not an option in a semi-continuous system. To apply this algorithm to the systems of this thesis it was therefore necessary that the models of both source and target language are defined on the same codebook. Thus the Model Merging basically reduces to a weighted combination of GMM weight vectors of different states and can be implemented very fast. However, the addition of Gaussians across languages is no longer included in this Model Merging algorithm, and thus the efficiency is probably reduced.

4.6.5   HMM Adaptation

In the setting of this thesis, two different adaptations are possible. First, the HMM models could be adapted to an accent group of speakers. Second, the models could be adapted to individual speakers. Due to the individual aspects accents can have, the second approach could probably give better recognition rates. However, for a real in-car system it would be necessary for the second approach to automatically identify speakers. Realizing such an automatic speaker identification and adaptation approach was the topic of another PhD thesis that was undertaken in parallel to this thesis at HBAS[Herb 10]. The other option of performing unsupervised adaptation to a speaker has the problem that the system either looses the learned adaptation with every restart of a car, or the system might become unusable for other speakers.

Therefore the first approach is considered here, and an adaptation to accent groups is analyzed. In this case, the adaptation has anyway to be performed offline. This means the amount of adaptation data is not as relevant as usual, as anyway a couple of speakers need to be recorded in order to prevent a dominance of one speaker with a non standard accent. Thus, if adaptation data is available, at least a couple of hours are available. This means that it is not necessary that the adaptation algorithm can work well with few data. Therefore, the models were adapted with the standard Baum-Welch training algorithm (see Section 2.3.4).

The performed experiments should show large improvements, as these are the only experiments that actually see training or development data that matches the test condition closely. However, it should be clear that these retraining adaptations are by far the most expensive adaptations, as they require development data for each accent. If 20-30 languages are targeted, data collections for up to 900 accents had to be made.

4.7   Summary

This chapter has described the systems and algorithms that are applied in the experiments. Section 4.1 introduced the general architecture of the HBAS speech recognizer, especially the training of the acoustic model for one language. These monolingual systems are also the benchmark systems for proposed multilingual acoustic models. The baseline for the new approaches is an acoustic model that keeps the codebook of the main language. The drawback of the benchmark system is that it requires more resources for the recognition of more languages, and the drawback of the baseline system is that it increased the training effort and performs significantly worse than benchmark systems.

The first algorithm that was proposed in this thesis dealt with the performance reduction. The performance is increased through the application of Multilingual Weighted Codebooks (MWCs) that have a better coverage for more languages. The basic idea is that the most divergent Gaussians from the codebooks of other languages are added to the codebook of the main language to reduce vector quantization errors.

Several possible distances measures are introduced, and a technique for the increased reusability of the MWCs is suggested.

The second algorithm was concerned with the training effort, that is increased significantly already with the baseline systems, and intractable for more than a couple of languages with the MWC approach. The idea of the on-the-fly generation of multilingual acoustic models is to replace the standard training of mixture weights for the emission probabilities of HMMs by an projection between Gaussian spaces. This is possible in a multilingual scenario, as mixture weights for each HMM have to be estimated repeatedly, and these repeated estimations can be replaced by a projection from the monolingual codebook of the corresponding language to any other codebook. This section suggested seven algorithms for the actual projection, an overview of them was given in Section 4.4.4.

The combination of the previous two algorithms leads to a scalable architecture. Section 4.5 explained why such a combination should have fruitful effects and showed a graphical representation of the process that combines these two algorithms for two tasks that are of primary interest for multilingual speech recognition.

Finally, a multilingual system also has to handle non-native speech as well as possible. Section 4.6 presented five algorithms that could be useful for that endeavor. The goal of the first algorithm is to determine the spoken language and/or the accent of the speaker through codebook share rates. The second algorithm modifies the self loop probabilities of HMM states to account for the fact that non-native speakers speak slower. The third algorithm modifies the variances of Gaussians with the aim to increase the importance of frequency bands that are less affected by non-native accent. The fourth algorithm combines models from the spoken and the native language of the speaker to new models that should match the non-native pronunciations of such speakers. The last algorithm modifies the HMM state emission probabilities with Baum-Welch iterations on non-native development data.

Chapter 5

Resources

5.1 Non-native Speech Databases

5.1.1 Problem

In order to work on speech recognition of non-native accented speech, non-native accented speech is needed. It has been said already that this is a problem, as there are no standard databases available. At the beginning of this thesis it seemed that there are only a couple of databases and all of them are significantly different from the command oriented speech recognition task this thesis is focused on. Unlike other research works in this field, the author chose to first analyze the literature for available databases before collecting a special database. The outcome of this review was encouraging, there were already a lot of collections, and some even close to the desired target domain.

Nevertheless, there is still far to few data for really generating specific models for all accents. Therefore the motivation for this thesis, to improve non-native speech recognition without additional data remained valid. Still some non-native data is needed, at least for tests of the proposed methods. If enough data is available, adaptation methods can be tried as well. Unfortunately, speech databases are always designed for special application domains. This leads to the fact that one databases is not sufficient for a language. There are databases for read text, command oriented speech, broadcast speech, meeting speech and so on. For non-native speech, this problem is multiplied by further factors, like the language proficiency, and of course the native language background of the speaker.

These and other factors were discussed in Section 3.4, for convenience the summarizing figure is repeated here (Figure 5.1).

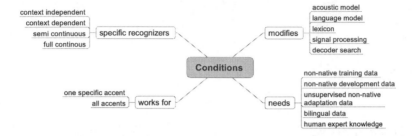

Figure 5.1: Conditions related to non-native techniques

In this work, the goal is non-native speech recognition for spoken interaction with devices in automobiles. The main focus is on interaction with telephone, radio and the navigation system. Possible further applications are sound system interaction, mp3 player control and Internet access.

All these applications focus on command oriented speech. Another aspect is that typical non-native speech in cars consists of geographical close origins of the languages or of combination with the world language English. Language pairs which match these two attributes are from now on referred to as in-domain language pair.

To summarize, the main points are listed in the following list

- Simple, command and task oriented speech

- Good quality of speech signal, no severe background noise to concentrate on non-native speech

- Maybe some recording in car to detect noise dependencies

- In general in-domain language pairs

In Section 5.1.2 an overview of the databases identified by the review is given. Section 5.1.3 presents detailed information about some of the larger and more interesting databases. Section 5.1.4 identifies some of the categories for which databases do exist. In Section 5.1.5, the conclusion is drawn that the existing databases are good enough, and the effort for collecting a new one is not needed.

5.1.2 Overview of Non-native Databases

This section presents an overview of non-native speech databases. The author does not claim that the following table contains all existing databases. For example, there are some meeting/presentation databases that are not contained. These special databases are regarded as being less relevant, as the speech they contain is difficult due to a variety of different influences what makes it hard to concentrate solely on non-native speech recognition. Apart from these databases, the table provides details about all databases the author was able to identify from publications.

The main table gives the following information about each corpus: The name of the corpus, the institution where the corpus can be obtained, or at least further information should be available, the language which was actually spoken by the speakers, the number of speakers, the native language of the speakers, the total amount of non-native utterances the corpus contains, the duration in hours of the non-native part, the date of the first public reference to this corpus, some free text highlighting special aspects of this database and a reference to another publication. The reference in the last field is in most cases to the paper which is especially devoted to describe this corpus by the original collectors. In some cases it was not possible to identify such a paper. In these cases the paper where the author first found information about this corpus is referenced.

Some entries are left blank and others are marked with unknown. The difference here is that blank entries refer to attributes the author was not able to find information about. Unknown entries, however, indicate that no information about this attribute is available in the database itself. As an example, in the Jupiter weather database [Live 99] no information about the origin of the speakers is given. Therefore this data is less useful for verifying accent detection or similar issues.

Where possible, the name is a standard name of the corpus, for some of the smaller corpora, however, there was no established name and hence an identifier had to be created. In such cases the name is a combination of the institution and the collector of the database.

When the databases contain native and non-native speech the table lists only attributes of the non-native part of the corpus. Most of the corpora are collections of read speech. If the corpus instead consists either partly or completely of spontaneous utterances, this is mentioned in the *Specials* column.

In the table of non-native databases some abbreviations for language names are used. They are listed in Table 5.1. The actual table with information about the different databases is shown in Table 5.2. The author also created a companion

website at Wikipedia [Raab 08a]. Everybody is invited to add missing information
for the benefit of all interested researchers.

Arabic	A	Japanese	J
Chinese	C	Korean	K
Danish	D	Malaysian	M
Dutch	Dut	Norway	N
English	E	Portugese	P
French	F	Russian	R
German	G	Spanish	S
Greek	Gre	Swedish	Swe
Indonesian	Ind	Thai	T
Italian	I	Vietnamese	V

Table 5.1: Abbreviations for languages used in the table of databases.

Corpus	Author	Available at	Language(s)	#Speakers	native Language	#Utt.	Dur.	Date	Specials	Reference
AMI		EU	E		Dut and others		100h		meetings	[AMI 07]
ATR-Gruhn	Gruhn	ATR	E	96	C G F J Ind	15000		2004	proficiency rating	[Gruh 04a]
BAS Strange Corpus I+II		BAS	G	139	50 countries	7500		1998		[Univ 98]
Broadcast News		LDC	E					1997		[Tomo 01a]
Berkeley Restaurant		ICSI	E	55	G I H C F S J	2500		1994		[Jura 94]
Cambridge-Witt	Witt	U. Cambridge	E	10	J I K S	1200		1999		[Witt 99a]
Cambridge-Ye	Ye	U. Cambridge	E	20	C	1600		2005		[Ye 05]
Children News	Tomokiyo	CMU	E	62	J C	7500		2000	spontaneous	[Tomo 01a]
CLIPS-IMAG	Tan	CLIPS-IMAG	F	15	C V		6h	2006		[Tan 06]
CLSU		LDC	E	64	22 countries	5000		2007	telephone	[Land 07]
CMU		CMU	E		G	452	0.9h		not available	[Wang 03]
Cross Towns	Schaden	U. Bochum	6 countries	161	E F G I S	72000	133h	2006	city names	[Scha 06a]
Duke-Arslan	Arslan	Duke U.	E	93	15 countries	2200		1995	telephone speech	[Arsl 97]
ERJ	Minematsu	U. Tokyo	E	200	J	68000		2002		[Mine 02]
Fischer		LDC	E		many		200h		telephone speech	[Cier 04]
Fraenki	Fitt	U. Edinburgh	F I N Gre	10	G	700		1995	city names	[Fitt 95]
Hispanic		U. Erlangen	E	19	S	2148	20h			[Stem 01]
IBM-Fischer	Byrne	IBM	E	22	S F G I	2000		1998	spontaneous	[Byrn 98]
ISLE	Atwell	EU/ELDA	E	40	G I	4000		2002	digits	[Fisc 03]
Jupiter	Zue	MIT	E	46	unknown		18h	2000		[Menz 00]
K-SEC	Rhee	SiTEC	E	unknown	K	5146		1999	telephone speech	[Live 99]
LDC WSJ1		LDC	E	336		800	1h	2004		[Rhee 04]
MIST		ELRA	E F G	10	Dut	2200		1996		[Amda 00], [TNO 07]
NATO Hiwire		NATO	E	75	F Gre I S	8100		2007	clean speech	[Segu 07]
NATO M-ATC	Pigeon	NATO	E	81	F G I S	9833	17h	2007	background noise	[Pige 07]
NATO N4		NATO	E	622	unknown		7.5h	2006	background noise	[Bena 99]
Onomastica			11 countries	115		(121000)		1995	only lexicon	[Onom 95]
PF-STAR		U. Erlangen	E	57	G	4627		2005	children speech	[Hack 07]
Sunstar		EU	E	100	G S I P D		3.4h	1992	multiple data sets	[Teix 97]
TC-STAR	Heuvel	ELDA	E S	unknown	EU countries	40000	13h	2006	parliament speech	[Heuv 06]
TED	Lamel	ELDA	E	40(188)	many		10h	1994	Eurospeech 93	[Lame 94]
TLTS		DARPA	A		E		1h	2004		[Mote 04]
Tokyo-Nishina		U. Tokyo	J	140	10 countries	35000		2004		[Nish 04]
Verbmobil		U. Munich	E	44	G		1.5h	1994	very spontaneous	[Wahl 00]
VODIS		EU	F G	178	F G	2500		1998	car navigation	[Tran 99]
WP Arabic	Rocca	LDC	A	35	E			2002		[LaRo 02]
WP Russian	Rocca	LDC	R	26	E	800	1h	2003		[LaRo 03]
WP Spanish	Morgan	LDC	S		E	2500	2h	2006		[Morg 06]

Table 5.2: Table of non-native speech databases.

5.1.3   Details for Selected Databases

CSLU

This database is special because of its wide variety of non-native accents (22 non-native accents). The corpus contains utterances of foreign speakers that were asked to speak about themselves in English for 20 seconds. The recordings were conducted over telephone. A strength of this corpus is that it contains human judgments of the level of foreign accent on a level from one to four. 5000 utterances with each 20 seconds result in a estimated corpus size of almost 30 hours.

This corpus is available through LDC.

CrossTowns

The strength of this corpus is that it covers many language directions (speakers of one native language speaking another language). Altogether the corpus covers 24 different language directions. Each recording of a language direction contains two times 45 city names per speaker. First the 45 city names are read from a prompt, and then they are repeated after listening to the name via headphone. 13000 of the utterances are manually transcribed at the phonetic level, and there is information about the language proficiency of the speakers.

A planned release at ELRA in 2006 did not succeed. According to the author of the corpus a future release of this corpus is undetermined.

NATO Hiwire

This corpus contains speech from 81 different speakers. The utterances were collected in a military pilot-ground control conversation task. An advantage for general speech recognition of this corpus is that is was originally collected in a studio and only later convolved with typical cockpit noise. As a consequence, the corpus now contains two signal levels, one clean speech and one with added noise. This corpus was available for free to researchers, and might still be. For more information, it is suggested to contact one of the authors of [Segu 07].

CLIPS-IMAG

This corpus differs from other corpora because of its untypical combination of languages. Whereas most databases focus on English as foreign language, this corpus contains French non-native speech by Vietnamese and Chinese speakers. With a total amount of 6h of non-native speech this corpus is also relatively large. The speech covers dialogues and articles from the tourist domain. Although this makes the nature of the sentences spontaneous, the data is read speech. For information if and how this corpus can be obtained it is recommended to contact the authors of [Tan 06].

ATR-Gruhn

Another corpus which has the advantage of proficiency ratings of the speakers. The corpus contains 89 non-native speakers of English, their origin is distributed between speakers from China, France, Germany, Indonesia and Japan. Additionally, there are seven more speakers with other native languages.

Each speaker read 25 credit card number sequences, 48 phonetically rich sentences and six hotel reservation dialogs. The proficiency rating was performed by native English speakers from the US and Canada with teaching experience. Each utterance was judged by three to four raters who assigned a score from one(best) to five(worst). This database is available at ATR (or its successor NICT).

ISLE

ISLE is one of the largest corpora (measured in hours) and has the advantage to be distributed by ELDA for a moderate price. There are only two accents, German and Italian accented English in this corpus. The speakers read 1300 words of a non-fictional, autobiographic text and 1100 words in short utterances which were designed to cover typical pronunciation errors of language learners. The corpus is annotated at the word and at the phone level, which makes it especially interesting for the development of Computer Assisted Language Learning systems. This corpus is available through ELDA.

ERJ

ERJ (English read by Japanese) is a large corpus which contains utterances from Japanese speakers that read English text. This corpus was collected with the intention to support CALL research for language learning. Therefore the corpus provides elaborated pronunciation scores with the spoken utterances. The pronunciation of each student is rated regarding segmental, rhythmic and intonational aspects by native English language teachers. The corpus is available at [Spee 02].

5.1.4 Categories of Databases

In many cases potential users of these databases will have a clear understanding of what system they want and what they want to do with it. Systems can for example be speech recognizers, text to speech systems, pronunciation trainers or computer assisted language learning systems. The task might be to train, to adapt or only to test a system. Example applications are navigation devices, military communications, presentation systems or language learning systems. Therefore, it is interesting to analyze for what categories or tasks there are already databases.

Speech operated Navigation Devices

Navigation devices, as most mobile devices still have to cope with limited computing power. Therefore systems running on these devices are less elaborated and usually only cover a restricted, command oriented user interface.

Of course, of major interest for navigation devices are city and street names as well as digits, for example for street numbers or postal addresses. Hence, a very interesting corpus for this task would be the CrossTowns corpus, as it covers mainly city names in a couple of languages. As it is not yet available, two further corpora are suitable with restrictions: the CLIPS-IMAG and the ISLE corpus. The CLIPS-IMAG corpus has the advantage of covering the tourist domain, which is likely to contain similar places of interest as they will be demanded from navigation devices. The disadvantage of this corpus is, that it covers more or less exotic language combinations, that are unlikely to be in the focus of commercial products in the next years. Finally, the ISLE corpus. Compared to the other suggestions, it has the disadvantage not to contain in-domain data. Yet about half of the corpus are simple and short utterances, which is similar to the simple command interaction current navigation systems can handle.

Military Communications

This application area has the advantage that recently a couple of interesting corpora became available (see Section 5.1.3). The M-ATC (Military Air Traffic Control) corpus covers pilot controller communications with a variety of accents, strong background noise and a high number of different speakers. The N4 corpus contains recordings from naval communication training sessions in the Netherlands. The transcriptions of the N4 corpus are very rich regarding information about speaker background. The Hiwire corpus finally contains spoken pilot orders that are input for the Controller Pilot Data Link Communications [Fede]. An advantage of this corpus compared to the two other ones is that the recordings were originally made in a studio. Thus this corpus provides clean speech as well as noisy speech which was obtained through convolution of clean speech and noise. The Hiwire and M-ATC corpus have the additional advantage to be free of charge for European researchers.

Speech operated Presentation Transcription Systems

There are two databases that are likely to be useful for this application, namely TC-STAR and TED. The TC-STAR corpus contains about 100 hours of Spanish and English transcribed parliament speech each. As listed in Table 5.2, this reduces to 11 hours of non-native English and some amount of non-native Spanish in both training and test corpora of TC-STAR. A larger part of the TC-STAR corpus is from non-native interpreters. As it is not clear to what extent speech from an interpreter relates to standard non-native speech the non-native interpreter part is not included in Table 5.2. The Translanguage English Database (TED) is a corpus which contains almost all presentations from the Eurospeech 1993. The speech material totals 47 hours, however only about 10 hours are transcribed. Due to the typical mixture of presentations from a variety of countries, it is believed that a large amount of the presentations is given with non-native accents.

Computer Assisted Language Learning Systems

Most speech technologies only need orthographic transcriptions for the databases to train systems. This is different for CALL systems. In order to detect and/or classify mispronunciation it is useful to have judgments of pronunciation quality and/or a transcription at the phonetic level. Corpora which can provide proficiency ratings are the ISLE, Cross Towns, ATR-Gruhn, ERJ, Tokyo-Kikuko and CLSU corpus. Of these corpora, the ISLE and Cross Towns corpus contain also transcriptions at the phonetic level.

5.1.5 Summary

Section 5.1.4 has showed that there are databases that are well suited for non-native speech recognition. Especially, the CrossTowns corpus would be very good (see Section 5.1.3). Unfortunately, it is still not publicly available. Most other databases differ in one of the following aspects from the data that is needed for this thesis.

- Difficult phonetically rich sentences, which do not cover the needed simple command oriented speech sufficiently

- Exotic language combinations, like Vietnamese French, which are scarce and not in the main interest

- Recording conditions which are extremely spontaneous and with extreme background noise

After the comparison of the desired attributes, and a check for availability, two existing databases remained. The ISLE and the Hiwire corpora. The ISLE corpus is available at ELDA for 1500 Euro for commercial use. It contains 18 hours of non-native English from 23 Germans and 23 Italians. The Hiwire corpus contains non-native English from 81 speakers from four different countries. It also seemed to be repeated effort to collect another small database, if a very good database already exists with the CrossTowns database. Especially, as the collection of a new database, even a small one, is a considerable effort regarding both organizational complexity and costs.

Considering all this aspects, the author decided not to collect a new database. As the next section shows, both the Hiwire and the ISLE copora were acquired for the necessary tests. As a benefit of that more time remained for work on the algorithms that are presented in this thesis.

5.2   Naming Scheme

As mentioned in Section 1.1.3 one problem this thesis has to deal with is the multitude of systems that are possible. Hence the experimental section has to evaluate many different trained HMM model sets in order to prove the effectiveness of the algorithms in all cases. To keep track of which system was used where, the following internal naming scheme was applied.

LL	_	XXXX	_	LL	V	W
LID1		Codebook		LID2	Main version	Sub version

LID1 is the language code for the main language of the codebook in two letters, the codebook size is specified in four digits followed by the second LID2, that specifies the languages that are added. If one language is added, this is the name of the additional languages, if more languages are added just the number of added languages is indicated. Finally, the version of the system is specified. This version information specifies for example which dictionaries and which training data is used. Almost all the results presented in the experimental section of this thesis have the same main version (C), thus this information is less relevant for comparing the results in the experimental section.

To give examples, GE_1024 C1 means that the main language is German, the codebook has 1024 Gaussians and the other files are from version C. GE_1424_4L C1 means that the main language is German, the codebook has 1424 Gaussians and Gaussians have been added from 4 languages. In many figures and tables these exact names have been replaced by simpler identifiers, but in some cases where quite different systems are compared the exact names were maintained for clarity.

5.3 Training Data

Most of the recognizers are trained on Speecon data [Iskr 02]. The Speecon database contains similar data for 25 languages. Each language is collected with 4 different microphones. For the training in this thesis, only headset speech (channel 0) is used. The availability of similar collections for many languages was a key argument for the application of Speecon as training material.

Table 5.3 gives details about the size and the number of speakers of the Speecon training material. For each language each channel contains roughly 200 hours of speech. After segmentation this reduces to 80 hours of speech.

	GE	US	IT	FR	SP
Sentences	153k	151k	157k	157k	158k
Speakers	562	550	550	550	564

Table 5.3: Speecon training data

The Speecon training material has the advantage to have only low levels of background noise, but this is not the scenario for the actual products of Harman Becker. Many internal experiments have shown that it is better to use in-car data for training product classifiers, instead of using clean speech for training and then trying to remove the in-car noise of the test.

In order to prove that the algorithms work well for this scenario as well, sometimes classifiers were trained with in-house data. All the experiments made with this additional data came to the same conclusions as the presented experiments. However, only few of the these additional tests are presented in this thesis.

5.4 Development Data

Some experiments have been conducted with non-native development data. Utterances from two different databases are used for adaptation. The first four development sets are as specified in the Hiwire database [Segu 07]. Table 5.4 presents the details for them. The Hiwire development sets are non-overlapping with the Hiwire test sets, but they have the same speakers.

Development Set	# Speakers	# Words	# Utterances	Grammar
Italian	20	3450	993	140
French	31	5362	1550	140
Spanish	10	1750	500	140
Greek	20	3500	1000	140

Table 5.4: Development data from the Hiwire corpus

However, as most of the experiments are tested on data from the Hiwire corpus, the question was if the observed improvements are only due to adaptation to non-native speech, or if other issues like adaptation to the recording conditions did also improve the performance. Therefore 80% of the speech from the ISLE Corpus (Interactive Spoken Language Education, [Menz 00]) constitutes a second development set. The remaining 20% were kept as an additional test set. Due to the focus of language education, the ISLE data was collected in parts that focus on different linguistic aspects that are relevant for second language learners as listed in Table 5.5. The second column in this table indicates how many utterances of this block were spoken by each speaker.

Block	#Utterances	Linguistic issue	Examples
A	27	wide vocabulary	"The first important expedition was sent to
B	33	coverage	everest in nineteen twenty one."
C	22		
D	81	problem phones	"I said bad not bed."
		weak forms	"She's wearing a brown wooly hat and a red scarf."
E	63	stress	"The convict expressed anger at the sentence."
		weak forms	"The jury took two days to convict him."
		problem phones	
		consonant clusters	
F	10	weak forms	"I would like chicken with fried potatoes,
		problem phones	broccoli, peas and a glass of water."
G	11	weak forms	"This year I'd like to visit Rome for a few days."
		problem phones	

Table 5.5: Different linguistic parts of the ISLE corpus according to [Menz 00].

Altogether, the ISLE development set contained 4446 utterances of German speakers and 4207 utterances of Italian speakers. The German accented English test set contained 1170 utterances and the Italian accented test set 1107 utterances. To allow a reasonable recognition with a grammar based language model, the recognition grammar contained all sentences that were in the respective test set.

Test Set	# Speakers	# Words	# Utterances	Grammar
GE_City	161	2005	1763	2498
US_City	33	852	657	500
US_Digits	48	12145	3696	10
US_Navi	33	1646	893	50000
IT_City	41	2000	2000	2000
FR_City	206	3308	1982	2000
SP_City	103	5143	3672	3672
Hiwire_IT	20	3482	990	140
Hiwire_FR	31	5192	1549	140
Hiwire_SP	10	1759	499	140
Hiwire_GR	20	3526	1000	140
IFS_MP3wk	96	831	285	63
ISLE_GE	23	12665	1170	1170
ISLE_IT	23	12226	1107	1107

Table 5.6: Description of test sets. The upper part describes the native test sets and the lower part the non-native tests.

5.5 Test Data

In this thesis many different tests are needed. The experiments work with multilingual classifiers, therefore tests for every language are needed. Furthermore, tests have to be performed for as many different non-native accents as possible, as each non-native accent is different.

In the upper part of Table 5.6 the details for the native tests are specified. These tests are performed on in-house data and vary in the signal quality. This issue leads to the impression that some languages have higher recognition rates than other languages. Most of the tests are city names, but for English also sometimes digits and addresses (navi test) are tested.

The non-native test sets are mostly performed on Hiwire. An important aspect for this test is that the same speakers are in the Hiwire development set. This was not a design choice of this work, but is due to the split in development and test sets as supplied with the data. Typical utterances in Hiwire are presented below.

```
can accept
$v $h $f one one four three
modify
select $h $f two three four nine six
arc mode
```

The non-native test IFS_MP3wk is from an internal data collection of song titles spoken by Germans. The wk stands for with keyword. This means each speaker added a keyword like album, song or title in front of the actual name. For example, to listen to Eros Ramazotti, the correct utterance is Interpret Eros Ramazotti. Details for these tests are specified in the lower part of Table 5.6. The Hiwire database contains English speech from French, Greek, Spanish and Italian speakers. Only the IFS_MP3wK test tests on Italian, French and Spanish artists names.

The general naming scheme for test sets is that native test sets start with the language that is spoken followed by the actual name of the test. For non-native tests, first the name of the test is given, followed by the native language of the speakers. This works well for the non-native test sets, as the spoken language in the tests in this thesis is in most cases English.

5.6   Summary

This chapter has covered two different aspects. First it has analyzed and discussed available databases for non-native speech. The rest of this chapter then described in detail the data that was used for the experiments.

The first part started with the explanation why it is difficult to have the appropriate data at hand for non-native speech recognition. After this an overview of available databases was given. The most relevant of these databases for this thesis were discussed. The databases were also categorized, to make it easier for other researchers to find an appropriate database.

Based on the findings from the first part, the best available data was selected for the actual experiments in this thesis. Due to the variety of different experiments a naming scheme was defined to have unique names for the performed experiments. However, for the ease of reading the exact names are replaced by simpler names in the experimental section whenever this is possible without the loss of relevant information. The other three sections then specified the training, development and test data.

Chapter 6

Experiments

6.1 Monophones vs. Triphones

This section compares monophones and triphones for non-native speech recognition. In the literature the dominating opinion is that monophones are better for non-native speech [Gruh 04b, He 01]. However, to the best knowledge of the author no paper did yet compare monophones with triphones with different amounts of training data for non-native speech recognition. This is an important aspect as it is clear that triphones can benefit more from additional training data than monophones. Our results prove this common knowledge.

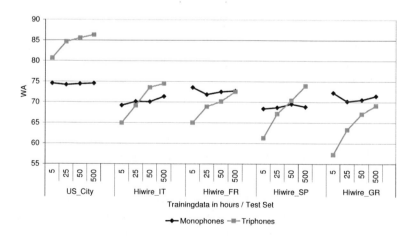

Figure 6.1: Comparison of monophones vs. triphones with different amounts of training data

Figure 6.1 shows the performance for native and non-native speech as more training data is added. In order to have more training data available Harman internal training data was used. Tests are performed with 5, 25, 50 and 500 hours of training data, the test sets are the native US cities test and non-native tests from the Hiwire database.

The triphone acoustic model with 500 hours performs similar for French and Greek, but is clearly better for Spanish and Italian accented English. Although the amount of training data is increased by two magnitudes, the monophone acoustic models do not benefit from additional training data for all test sets. For the triphone systems, the benefit of additional training data is clear, both the performance on the native and non-native tests increases significantly. For the native US city test triphones outperform monophones already with 5 hours, and continue to get better with more training data. For the non-native tests, monophones are significantly better for few training data. The low absolute numbers in Figure 6.1 are due to a channel mismatch between the training data and the non-native test sets.

To verify the result that well trained triphones can outperform monophones for non-native speech with matching channel conditions, another experiment was performed with recognizers trained on Speecon data that were adapted to the Hiwire channel conditions via retraining on the Hiwire development set. The results in Figure 6.2 agree with the previous results, all four accents are better recognized by the triphone system. More details about these results are given in Section 6.5.5. To conclude, both Figure 6.1 and 6.2 support the idea that well trained triphones can be better than monophones for non-native speech recognition. Therefore, the following experiments are all performed with triphones. Another reason for this is that triphone acoustic models offer more possibilities for the adaptation to non-native speech as more parameters can be adapted.

6.2   Multilingual Weighted Codebooks

The next sections describe experiments that analyze the effects of MWCs and answer some of the design questions that have to be regarded during the construction of MWCs. For these experiments Speecon data is used. Some experiments are performed only with a bilingual German/English recognizer, others are performed on five languages (German, English, Spanish, French and Italian).

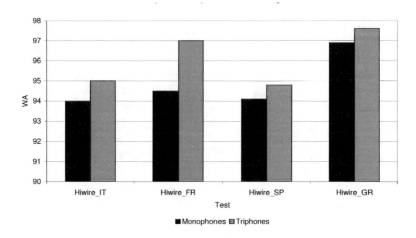

Figure 6.2: Comparison of monophones vs. triphones after retraining

6.2.1 Distance Metrics

The acoustic models are trained as described in Section 4.2. They differ in the codebook for the vector quantization. The baseline system is the acoustic model with only the German codebook. All further results are from MWCs that are constructed as described in Section 4.3.2. Figure 6.3 illustrates the performance gains that are achieved with three different distance measures on an English test set: LVM for Log Variance Minimization, KLD for Kullback Leibler Divergence and MAH for the Mahalanobis distance. Each distance is evaluated for two different codebook sizes, in the first case there are 76 Gaussians added and in the second case 176 Gaussians are added to the German codebook.

The leftmost and the rightmost bar indicate the baseline and the maximum performance that can be achieved if actually all Gaussians of both languages were used. In this case actually a slightly different English codebook was applied that had only 768 Gaussians. This codebook was used for initial experiments and was built on more training data. However, as in the next sections many different codebook sizes were needed, the codebook training was then consistently restricted to Speecon data. The different bars show that all distances work well as they achieve around 40% of the maximum improvement when only 10% of the additional Gaussians are added and up to 65% of the maximum improvement when only about 20% of the English Gaussians are added to the German codebook.

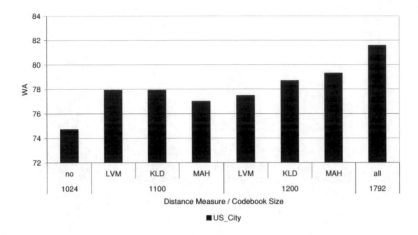

Figure 6.3: Different distance metrics on an English test set

In Figure 6.4 another experiment is performed to verify that none of the distance measures has a negative influence on the main language. Therefore the same recognizers are used to recognize a German test set. The results are satisfying, as the performance is always slightly over the performance of the baseline system. The improvements are probably due to the fact that the acoustic model now has in total more parameters than the baseline system.

None of the distance measures outperformed the others significantly, however to reduce the number of necessary experiments in later sections, the Mahalanobis distance was chosen as it provided the best recognition accuracy for the test with 1200 Gaussians. It should be noted that the absolute numbers in this section are not comparable to later sections as they were partly trained on additional data.

6.2.2   Codebook Size

This second set of experiments evaluates the effect of different final sizes of the codebook. The results are shown in Table 6.1. The size of the MWCs is varied as indicated in the top row. Each MWC contains 1024 Gaussians from the German codebook and a varying amount of Gaussians from the English codebook. The first test is from Germans who speak German and the other three test sets are English by native English speakers.

The different kind of test sets have to be analyzed separately. The performance on the German test is almost unaffected by the size of the MWC. However, the addition

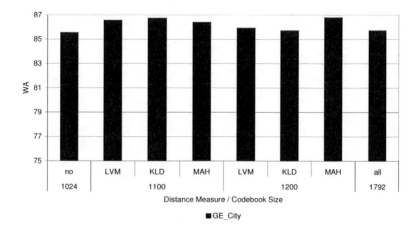

Figure 6.4: Different distance metrics on a German test set

1024 GE + US. Gaus.	0	26	76	126	176	276	1024
GE_City	84.1	84.3	84.9	**85.0**	84.7	84.4	82.9
US_City	67.3	67.8	69.3	72.0	72.5	73.4	**74.5**
US_Digits	96.6	96.8	96.9	97.2	97.3	97.2	**97.7**
US_Navi	47.9	50.7	51.8	53.1	53.7	55.1	**56.0**

Table 6.1: Effects of MWC size with additional US Gaussians. The horizontal line in the table separates the German from the English test sets.

of all Gaussians reduced the performance slightly. This is probably due to the fact that there are now many redundant Gaussians in the codebook. Nevertheless, for the MWC systems the aim that the multilingual recognizer performs as well on the main language as before is achieved.

The performance on the native English test sets gets significantly better the more English Gaussians are added to the MWC. The relationship between the codebook size and the performance is visualized in Figure 6.5. The figure shows that already few extra vectors yield a high share of the possible improvement. The small drop in performance for the digit test from 176 to 276 additional Gaussians can be ignored as it is only 0.1 in absolute WA. Therefore adding Gaussians to the MWC has been shown to be an effective method to handle multilinguality.

One possible criticism about to the results is that the improvements could be only due to the increased size of the codebook or that a monolingual acoustic model with as many Gaussians as an MWC will perform better on the main language. The

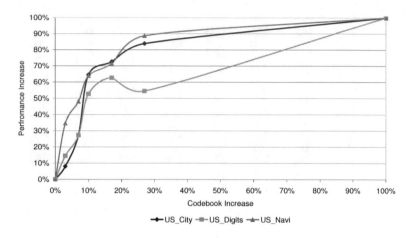

Figure 6.5: Relative improvements on English data with MWC

GE Gaussians	1024	1050	1100	1150	1200	1300	2048
GE_Speecon	83.3	**83.8**	83.3	83.4	83.2	83.6	83.6
GE_City	84.1	84.1	84.4	**84.6**	84.4	84.1	83.8
US_City	67.3	66.2	66.2	66.3	65.9	66.8	**67.8**
US_Digits	96.6	96.6	96.5	96.5	96.4	96.4	**96.8**
US_Navi	47.9	**48.4**	45.0	46.4	46.5	47.1	46.5

Table 6.2: Effects of size of monolingual codebooks.

results in Table 6.2 show that there is no performance increase when more Gaussians are allowed for German. The acoustic models in this section vary again slightly from systems in later sections and the numbers cannot be compared to results from other sections.

To summarize, this section showed two aspects. First, it is always a trade off. The more Gaussians are allowed for each language, the better the overall performance, but more Gaussians also require more hardware resources. Yet, the results also showed that already few vectors can achieve large parts of the maximum possible improvement. Thus it is probably advisable to add at least some additional Gaussians. Second, the improvements are not just due to additional parameters in the acoustic model, as the recognition performance on English is not improved when larger codebooks are built solely on German speech.

6.2.3 Simplifications

The previous experiments only evaluated a bilingual German/English system. This section tests the faster provision of multilingual systems through LDA reload. For this set of experiments, German is the main language and English, Italian, French and Spanish are the additional languages. For each bilingual recognizer 100 Gaussians from the additional language were added according to their Mahalanobis distance to the German codebook.

	GE_City	US_City	IT_City	FR_City	SP_City
GE_1024 C1	84.1	67.3	85.2	68.7	88.3
GE_1124_* C1	84.1	69.8	86.7	72.6	89.4
LDA Reload	**84.2**	69.0	85.4	71.3	88.4
GE_1424_4L C1	84.0	**70.9**	**87.9**	**71.3**	**91.5**

Table 6.3: Baseline performance of only the German codebook, performance of bilingual MWCs with 100 additional Gaussians and two five-lingual MWC systems. One of them with LDA reload and one with the standard procedure that creates the codebook first and then trains all required languages.

Table 6.3 shows the results with LDA reload. The first row contains the baseline word accuracy scores (only the German codebook). The second row gives the scores of the bilingual systems, the star in the name of the system indicates that the system is different for each column. The third row contains the result of the five-lingual system with reloaded LDA, and the last one the result of a five-lingual recognizer trained without LDA reloading. The last recognizer will be describe more in detail in the next section.

Positive about these results is that each bilingual system improves the German codebook baseline. However, reloading the LDA gives significantly worse results than the standard training procedure. Therefore, for further results always the standard training procedure is used. It is also visible that Gaussians from other languages help in the majority of cases to improve over the performance of the bilingual system. This is seen when row 3 is compared with row 5.

6.2.4 Five-lingual System

This section incorporates findings from the previous sections and evaluates the influence of MWCs when more languages are considered. All acoustic models in this section are trained on Speecon data only. In a first experiment, German is considered as the main language and all Gaussians from the additional language codebooks are added to one large 4096 sized additional language codebook. From this codebook different amounts of Gaussians are added to the German codebook. This ensures a maximum average performance as the final codebook should cover all additional languages as well as possible.

Figure 6.6 shows the results, the 1424 system is the one that was already mentioned in Table 6.3. The differences between the test sets are not relevant, as they are caused by different noise conditions for the different test sets as well as by different inherent difficulties of the languages for ASR. It is the tendency of each curve in itself that is important. The performance for all tests of the additional languages improves significantly when MWCs are used. The tendency is mostly as expected, the larger the codebook the better the performance. The performance on English is increased from 65.6% to 72.0% WA and on Italian from 85.2% to 89.7% WA. The first curve shows that the performance on the German test set varies insignificantly. This is as expected, as the LBG produces already an optimal codebook for German. Thus the extensions to the codebook can not improve performance on German, but do not hurt either.

The other aspect that is shown by Figure 6.6 is that the benchmark system always performs best. However, the benchmark system recognizes with the appropriate monolingual models for each language. Thus, to realize this performance on all five languages altogether 5120 Gaussians are needed. The figure shows that the MWC systems comes close to the performance of the benchmark system, but has reduced the number of parameters for the Gaussians by 72% for the 1424 system and still by 64% for the 1824 acoustic model. It can also be expected that the parameter reduction can be set higher if more than five languages are combined, as most human sounds are already covered by the first five languages.

One possible critique to the MWC algorithm is that the same could be achieved with standard methods for codebook generation. To refute this argument Table 6.4 compares the performance of the acoustic model with 1424 Gaussians from the previous set of experiments with a system that has also 1424 Gaussians. However, the codebook of the acoustic model was built only with an LBG approach and data from all languages was equally important. The results prove that the standard LBG algorithm generates a good codebook for all languages, however the German performance suffers significantly, which is an undesired behavior as this is the native language of the user.

Figure 6.7 presents similar results, however, this time with English as the main language. Again, all additional languages improve, especially Italian and French benefit from additional Gaussians. The performance on English is decreased a little bit, but English is also the smallest of the test sets and the decrease is still insignificant.

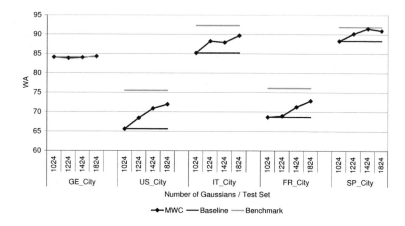

Figure 6.6: MWC performance starting from German codebook

Codebook	GE_City	US_City	IT_City	FR_City	ES_City
1424 MWC	**84.0**	**70.9**	87.9	71.3	**91.5**
1424 LBG	80.8	70.5	**90.6**	**72.2**	91.4

Table 6.4: Comparison to multilingual codebook created only with LBG.

6.2.5 Performance on Accented English

This section analyzes to what extent non-native speech recognition benefits from MWCs. The experiments are performed on non-native English with Spanish, French, Italian from the Hiwire database as well as on the IFS test that contains Italian, French and Spanish song titles. Figure 6.8 depicts the results for MWCs with different sizes and the performance of the benchmark system of each language.

As there is no monolingual acoustic model that can recognize the song titles from three different languages, no benchmark performance is given for this test. The MWCs contain for each test all Gaussians from the native language of the speaker, thus the MWCs that are tested on Hiwire_FR are not the same as the MWCs tested on Hiwire_IT. The results prove that this is the right decision, as all results consistently outperform the benchmark performance of a system with an English codebook. In fact, already the baseline is significantly better than the benchmark system. However, the graphs also indicate that no additional improvements are obtained through the MWCs.

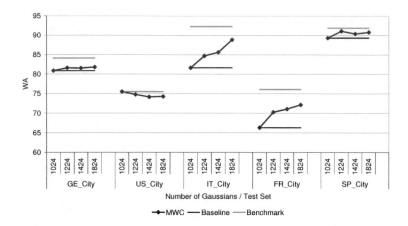

Figure 6.7: MWC performance starting from English codebook

To have further material for discussion monolingual codebooks of five languages
are tested on the four accents of the Hiwire data in Figure 6.9. The graphs indicate
two things. First, there is always a peak when the codebook of the main language of
the speakers is applied. Second, there is the general tendency that the more phonemes
a language has the better its performance on non-native English. In our phoneme
sets, which are based on standard SAMPA [Well 08] German has 59 Phonemes, Italian
50, English 46, French 37 and Spanish 29.

The only plot which does not directly show this tendency is the performance on
the Spanish accented English. In this case, however, it has to be considered that
the leftmost codebook with the fewest phonemes is also the native language of the
speakers. Therefore, in this graph the two influences work against each other, which
hides the effect of better performance when the codebook was built on a language
with more phonemes.

Table 6.5 gives the numbers from the graphs in Figure 6.9 as well as the performance for the native English city test. For this test, the same tendencies are observed.
The more phonemes the codebook generating language had, the better the performance of the codebook. However, as expected, in this case the influence of matching
conditions is stronger, the codebook that was built on English is significantly better
than all other codebooks for US_City.

The strongest contrast can be observed for the Spanish case. The Spanish codebook loses almost 20% absolute word accuracy on the native English test. On the
other hand, the Spanish codebook performs better than the English codebook for

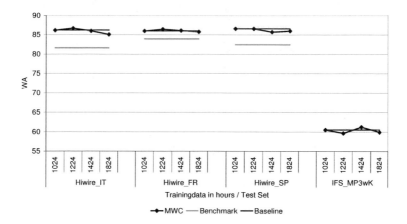

Figure 6.8: MWCs on non-native speech

Codebook	US_City	Hiwire_SP	Hiwire_FR	Hiwire_IT	Hiwire_GR
German	65.6	85.4	**86.9**	82.8	85.5
English	**75.5**	82.5	83.9	81.6	83.1
Italian	62.8	**87.1**	84.3	**86.2**	**86.5**
French	64.2	86.7	86.0	83.0	84.6
Spanish	56.1	85.5	79.6	80.0	82.9

Table 6.5: Word accuracies with native language codebooks. Each codebook has 1024 Gaussians.

English with Spanish accent. These results show how important it is to have a good codebook, and how strong non-native English differs from native English. The German and Italian codebook outperform the English codebook significantly for all non-native accents. This conclusion allows to say that MWCs can generate optimal codebooks for non-native speech as they can cover more phonemes than any monolingual codebook.

Apart from this unexpected aspect of non-native speech, the results also provide evidence for the common notion that non-native speakers use sounds of their mother tongue. The codebook built on the mother tongue of the speaker always performs very good, even if the language itself has fewer phonemes. The Spanish codebook system achieves 85.5% on the Spanish accented English, and the Italian codebook system achieves by far the best performance on the Italian accented speech.

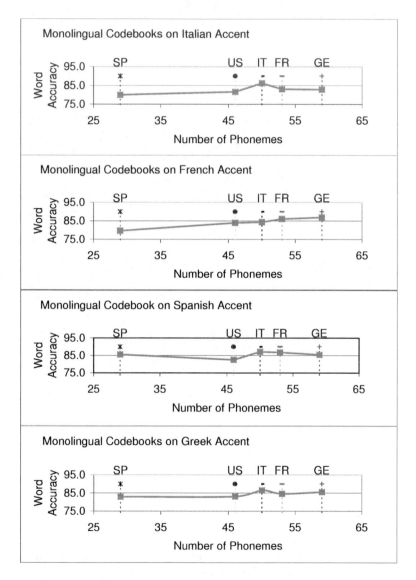

Figure 6.9: Native codebooks tested on different accents of English. The x-axis marker indicate the name of the language on which the codebook was built.

6.2.6 Summary

At first this section has evaluated several different distance metrics that could be appropriate for the generation of multilingual codebooks. The results did not show significant differences between the proposed distances, but the Mahalanobis distance has been chosen as the distance of choice for further experiments. It is also clear that larger codebooks can achieve more performance than smaller codebooks. These effects were analyzed in Section 6.2.2. The conclusion here was that a relatively small increase can already yield most of the possible improvement that would occur if all Gaussians from two languages were kept.

Section 6.2.3 explored a first idea how the combinatoric problem that comes with multilingual speech recognition could be alleviated. However, adding Gaussians from each added language separately did not yield comparable results as a global approach that tried to cover all additional languages as well as possible.

After these initial experiments, Section 6.2.4 evaluated the performance of MWCs on five different languages. The results demonstrate that the codebook coverage of foreign codebooks really is a problem for speech recognition, as MWCs could improve the performance on all languages significantly. These results are also valid in the scenario of this thesis, as one can assume that many people that drive frequently to destinations that are not in their home country have a solid knowledge of the language of this country. Thus their speech is less accented and close to the native speech that was tested in this section. The MWCs reduced the number of parameters compared to the benchmark system by 65% to 72% in this five-lingual setting.

This analysis was extended to stronger accented non-native speech in Section 6.2.5. A first finding of these experiments is that HMM models that are trained on native language codebooks are better than HMM models that are trained solely on the spoken language. The MWCs keep this improvement, but can not add further performance. However, altogether this means that MWCs are better than the baseline systems for almost fluent speakers, and better than the benchmark systems for less fluent speakers.

These findings are summarized in Table 6.6. The maintenance effort is probably not interesting from a research point of view. However, it is of paramount importance for a true realization of techniques in the a commercial product. It is quite likely that over the lifetime of a software system some changes occur in its runtime environment. The maintenance effort describes how much work is needed to adapt the sold systems to the new circumstances. The redundancy in the MWC systems is due to the fact that the acoustic models are trained for all combinations of languages.

	Languages	Effort	Perfor-mance	Maintenance
Monolingual Codebook (Baseline)	Can recognize all language combinations	n^2 training effort	Suboptimal perfor-mance	Hard to maintain (high redundancy)
MWC	Can recognize some language combinations	$> 2^n$ training effort	Good per-formance	Very hard to maintain (highest redundancy)

Table 6.6: Comparison of how many languages can be recognized, the training effort, the performance and finally the maintenance effort.

6.3   On-the-fly Multilingual HMMs

Section 6.2 showed that MWCs are a way to improve multilingual and non-native speech recognition in an embedded scenario. The other issues of multilingual speech recognition support are all related to the number of different systems that need to be supported and maintained. This section evaluates projections between HMMs as a possibility to increase the flexibility and to decrease the number of acoustic models needed. In contrast to all other projections, Projection 7 has a parameter that needs to be set to an appropriate value. Therefore, the next section determines a good setting of this parameter.

6.3.1   Combination Weight for Projection 7

This section evaluates the effect of different combination weights in Projection 7. Figure 6.10 shows that the exact value of this combination is not important, all weights in a range between 0.3 and 0.7 have approximately equal performance. The leftmost performance is the performance of only using the state projection, and the rightmost the performance of using only the Gaussian Projection. The combined performance is in all cases significantly better than each of the two other projections alone.

From these experiments a combination weight of 0.5 was chosen for the following experiments. However, this combination weight is adapted to put higher influence on the Gaussian distance when the otfMHMM algorithm is combined with the MWC algorithm in Section 6.4.

6.3.2   Comparing Projections

There are two attributes a projection should have. First, it should be executable on the embedded system, and second, it should be as efficient as possible. The first

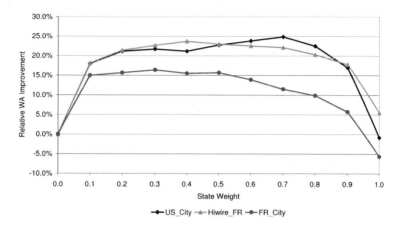

Figure 6.10: Influence of the combination weight in projection 7 on the performance on different test sets

attribute is achieved easier if elements that have to be computed only once for every language and do not depend on the actual combination are precomputed.

This means that for Projection 4 and 7 sorted lists are calculated that indicate which Gaussians to add from the additional language codebook. For Projection 5 and 7, similar lists are calculated that contain the closest states indices in each of the additional languages. Finally, for projection 6 lists that contain the closest HMMs are calculated.

The first column of Table 6.7 shows the word accuracy on the native US City test. The second column gives distances to the monolingual US English HMM models. The third column shows the runtime in seconds for precomputations. The fourth column shows the actual runtime of the estimation of the output probabilities of the HMM models. The runtime is given for the projection of one language with 1800 phoneme models to another codebook on an Intel Xeon dual core system with 3.6 GHz and two gigabyte RAM.

As expected, the optimal Projections 1-3 give by far the lowest error in L2 distance. However, Projection 1 results in a weight vector for the HMM states that is so different from regular probability distributions that a standard recognizer achieves only very low recognition rates. Projection 2 adds the normalization that weights have to sum to one, and this leads already to a reasonable recognition performance. Compared to other projections it is clear that the negative weights for some Gaussians still pose a problem for the decoding. Projection 3 gives the best overall performance,

Projection	WA	Distance L2	Precomp.	Runtime
Pro1	5.2	**4.08e-9**	330s	30s
Pro2	49.7	4.08e-9	330s	30s
Pro3	**55.5**	4.10e-9	330s	90s
Pro4	44.8	6.80e-8	2s	0.2s
Pro5	44.5	6.64e-8	12s	0.1s
Pro6	31.2	5.29e-8	4s	0.1s
Pro7	55.1	5.07e-8	14s	0.3s
Retrained	65.6	4.13e-8	-	14,400s

Table 6.7: Comparing mathematically optimal and approximated projections.

but is significantly slower than the approximated projections. These results show that none of the mathematically optimal projections is applicable for the proposed scalable architecture as the runtime will be too long on an embedded system.

Among the approximated projections, both Projection 4 (Gaussian mapping) and 5 (State mapping) achieve good performance in spite of their simplicity. Finally, Projection 7 (combined Gaussian + state mapping) has the best overall performance with both good recognition rate and fast runtime. The goal of the projections is to reduce the training complexity for multilingual recognition, not to increase the performance. The projections alone decrease performance, as shown in the last row of Table 6.7. Due to the fact that the approximated projections are much faster and that the best approximated projection achieves similar results as the L2 distance minimizing projections, in the following sections only the approximated projections 4-7 are considered further.

The runtime does of course depend on the system. At HBAS, the rule of thumb is that an embedded systems needs 20 times longer than a current desktop computer. This would increase the runtime of the approximated projections to a couple of seconds, compared to 30 minutes for every language with the mathematically motivated projection that gives correct probability distributions. Thus, the computation should be feasible on an embedded system for the approximations. In fact, in this case the rule of thumb might be an overestimation, as this rule is valid for the same code that runs on a desktop computer and on the embedded system. The measured code, however, is still object oriented. While this has advantages with respect to ease of programming and maintainability, it is probably far from computationally optimal.

6.3.3 otfMHMM on Native Speech

After important design questions have been answered by Section 6.3.1 and Section 6.3.2 the performance can be compared across different languages. The curves in Figure 6.11 depict that the behavior of the projection algorithms is similar on different languages. The different projections are actually sorted according to their average performance, thus projection 6 is the leftmost one and projection 7 the rightmost one. In all cases, the HMM based Projection 6 is worst and Projection 7 is the best. Of course, this is not true for the main language of the system. No changes are made here, and thus all systems perform equal. For the other languages, the best performance is in vicinity to the baseline, but still significantly below. So the

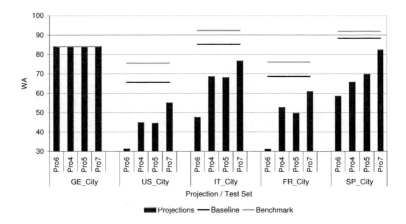

Figure 6.11: Performance of on-the-fly generated HMMs on native speech of different languages. The HMMs of the native recognizers were projected to the German codebook.

tendency is clear, the improved flexibility leads to reduced performance on native speech. Further experiments will show that these negative effects can be attenuated.

6.3.4 otfMHMM on Non-native Speech

Section 6.3.3 evaluated the effects on native speech, this section evaluates the influence on non-native speech. The systems in this section always use the native language of the speakers as main language. The curves in Figure 6.12 show the same behavior for the Hiwire tests as Figure 6.11 for the city names. Projection 6 is always worst, and Projection 7 always the best. Despite the fact that the speakers have different main language backgrounds the relative differences between the projections is similar for the three Hiwire tests. As in the native case, the best performance of the projections comes in the vicinity of the baseline, but is still significantly below.

However, the test with the Italian, French and Spanish song titles shows a different tendency. This is probably due to the fact that most of the speakers in this database have no knowledge at all about the language they are supposed to speak. One assumption is that they just apply the German pronunciation rules they are familiar with, which in fact causes many of their utterances to sound very German. It might be that the on-the-fly algorithms are actually doing a comparable mapping to German sounds, as they all perform close to the baseline system for this test.

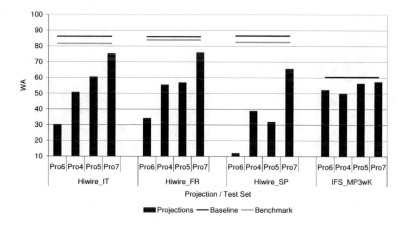

Figure 6.12: Performance of on-the-fly generated HMMs on non-native speech. The main language is the native language of the speakers, thus different for each test.

Projection 7 achieves 75.8% WA for Hiwire_FR and 75.2% for Hiwire_IT. The retrained acoustic models achieve 86.0% WA on the French accented part, and 86.2% on the Italian accented data. This performance difference has to regarded under the aspect that it takes less than one second to apply the projection algorithm and a couple of hours to do the Baum-Welch training.

6.3.5   Summary

The goal of the otfMHMM algorithm is to increase the flexibility of the speech recognition systems by allowing a combination of different languages on an embedded system. The goal of this section was to compare different methods that can achieve this. A first set of results already indicated that the projections based on L2 distance minimization proposed in Section 4.4.2 are no real option as their runtime on a desktop computer renders the actual application on an embedded system hardly feasible. The same section, however, showed that this is not fatal as the approximated projections can achieve similar performance with more desirable runtime.

After this initial decision, the approximated projections were evaluated on different languages and on different accents. The performance curves were in all cases very comparable, Projection 7 always performed best and in vicinity to acoustic models that were retrained with common Baum-Welch procedures. It is important to realize that a provision of such baseline systems for 20-30 languages is already at the border to being infeasible. Instead of the 20-30 monolingual systems, 400-900 systems are needed AND must be available on the actual embedded system. However, it is also clear that the performance drops are not desirable. To summarize, the main attributes of the otfMHMM algorithm are depicted in Table 6.8 and compared to the previous systems. The next section shows how the otfMHMM algorithm can be combined with the MWC algorithm to form an architecture that offers both flexibility and good performance.

	Languages	Effort	Performance	Maintenance
Monolingual Codebook (Baseline)	Can recognize all language combinations	n^2 training effort	Suboptimal performance	Hard to maintain (high redundancy)
MWC	Can recognize some language combinations	$> 2^n$ training effort	Good performance	Very hard to maintain (highest redundancy)
otfMHMM	Can recognize all language combinations	Almost none	Worst Performance	Very easy (no redundancy)

Table 6.8: Comparison of how many languages can be recognized, the training effort, the performance and finally the maintenance effort.

6.4 Scalable Architecture

The goal of this section is to evaluate the combination of the MWC and the otfMHMM algorithms. Section 6.3, especially Figure 6.11 revealed that the otfMHMM algorithm can perform in the same range as traditionally generated models, though the performance is still significantly below. From a theoretical viewpoint, the combination of the otfMHMM and the MWC algorithm should be very fruitful, as the otfMHMM algorithm has to perform bad when there are Gaussians that have no close counter-part in the new codebook. The MWC algorithm is tackling exactly this problem by adding the most different Gaussians to the new codebook. This section will show that the combination is not only promising in theory, but also in practice and that acoustic models generated with both algorithms can outperform systems that were built traditionally. Considering the otfMHMM algorithm, this section only reports results with Projection 4 and Projection 7, as they are the only Projections that depend on Gaussian proximity and can therefore benefit from a combination with the MWC algorithm.

6.4.1   Performance on Native Speech

The first set of experiments deals with native speech of the usual five languages. Figure 6.13 illustrates the significant benefits that come from a combination of the two algorithms when Projection 4 is applied. The more Gaussians are added to the codebook, the better the performance of the otfMHMM algorithm. As in most cases, a German codebook is the basis of the experiments and the baseline is the performance of HMMs trained conventionally with speech from five languages on the German codebook.

The picture visualizes that the on-the-fly generated acoustic models have the same performance as the conventional retrained system for three of the four additional languages with 400 additional Gaussians. This equal performance has the advantage of a fraction of calculation time for the provisioning of the acoustic model, but the disadvantage that more Gaussians are needed to achieve this performance. The Spanish test behaves significantly different than the other tests. This is probably due to the small phonetic inventory of the Spanish language (Section 6.2.5).

Projection 4 was consistently outperformed by Projection 7 in the experiments in Section 6.3.3. Figure 6.14 illustrates that the same is true for a combination with the MWC algorithm. With Projection 7, the baseline performance is achieved with 200 additional Gaussians. With 400 additional Gaussians, the baseline is outperformed for all additional languages.

To verify that these results are not just some peculiarity when a multilingual acoustic model is built starting from a German codebook, the same experiments are performed with English as main language. Due to the superior performance of Projection 7, only these results are presented here.

Figure 6.15 shows that the results are very similar to the results with the German codebook. Of course, as English is the main language this time no changes do occur for English, as the main language is always just the monolingual main language system.

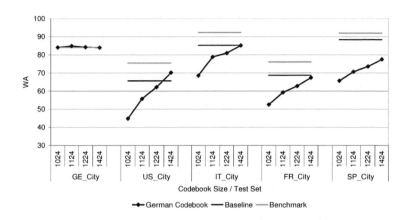

Figure 6.13: Scalable Architecture with Projection 4 on native test sets with German as main language

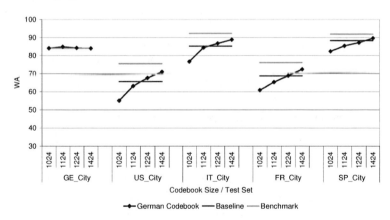

Figure 6.14: Scalable Architecture with Projection 7 on native test sets with German as main language.

For the additional languages the benefits of applying both MWC and otfMHMM are again clear.

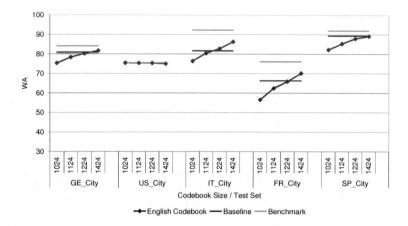

Figure 6.15: Scalable Architecture with Projection 7 on native test sets with English as main language.

In conclusion it can be said that the figures in this section demonstrated the fruitful effects of combining otfMHMM and MWC algorithm. In all cases equal performance to conventionally trained systems was achieved and in many cases the baseline was significantly outperformed. Furthermore the scalable architecture allows the support of any language combination.

6.4.2   Performance on Non-native Speech

Section 6.3.3 verified the benefits of a combination of MWC and otfMHMM for native speakers of a language. It was necessary to do these tests on the one hand because the range of languages that was covered was impossible to cover with non-native speech due to the lack of appropriate databases. On the other hand, considering one of the primary goals of providing speech recognition for a multilingual music jukebox, it could also be that users speak less accented when repeating artist names that they have heard frequently before.

But it remains necessary to test as much as possible on non-native speech to verify that the tendencies remain the same. Figure 6.16 illustrates the performance of Projection 4 for three Hiwire tests and the song title test. Each of the tests again uses a system that contains the full codebook of the native language of the speaker.

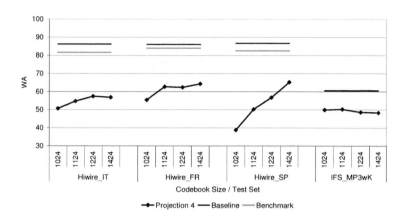

Figure 6.16: Scalable Architecture with Projection 4 on non-native test sets. The main language is the native language of the speakers, thus different for each test.

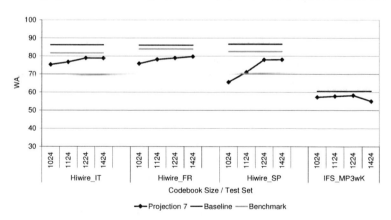

Figure 6.17: Scalable Architecture with Projection 7 on non-native test sets. The main language is the native language of the speakers, thus different for each test.

As in the native case, the otfMHMM performance improves when more Gaussians are added with the MWC algorithm. However, the curves are not as steep as for the tests on several native languages.

The same is true for results with Projection 7 in Figure 6.17. As in the native case, Projection 7 outperforms Projection 4 and is within reach to conventionally trained systems. However, for no non-native accent of English the performance of the projected models exceeds the trained models. The best relative performance is observed for Italian, where the benchmark WA is 81.6% and the otfMHMM algorithm achieves 78.8% WA with 400 additional Gaussians.

Nevertheless, both figures indicate that the combination of otfMHMM and MWC is also fruitful for non-native speech. Considering the drops in performance, they are probably in a reasonable range for real world customer products.

6.4.3   Runtime

This section discusses the runtime of the scalable architecture on an embedded system. The discussion will show that there are many aspects to consider, and there are different solutions, but the optimal solution will ultimately depend on the final architecture and resources of the embedded system. In the following discussion, the typical setup of this thesis with 1024 full covariance Gaussians for each monolingual codebook is assumed. This section is also mostly concerned with the time for the MWC creation, the creation of the appropriate HMM weights was discussed in Section 6.3.2.

The basic problem is that the generation of a codebook with the MWC algorithm takes some time. In fact, creating a bilingual MWC with 100 additional Gaussians takes 45 seconds and a five-lingual MWC with 100 additional Gaussians takes almost 180 seconds. The difference is that in the five-lingual case more Gaussians have to be considered as candidate for addition. These runtimes are measured on the desktop computer with 3.6 GHz. They are still far less than the time for a Baum-Welch training of HMM weights or a codebook generation from scratch, but probably unacceptable for an embedded system.

In the experiments in Section 6.4.1 and Section 6.4.2 this problem was avoided, as the list with Gaussians to be added was calculated once and then reloaded. In this way, the addition of 100 Gaussians was very fast. The number of lists is $n \cdot 2^{n-1}$, where n is the number of languages. The formula is not just 2^n, as each of the n languages can be the main language.

For 20 languages, 10 million lists are needed. Even if each list is saved with only the 500 best indices, and each index is saved as 2 byte short int, this would lead to

10 gigabyte of memory for all lists. This is probably not acceptable for an embedded system in the near future. However, for 10 languages only, 100,000 lists are needed. In this case the 10 megabyte of storage seem acceptable.

Yet, to determine which Gaussian to add is not the only problem. The other problem is to have the Gaussian in the right space to add. This problem is due to the LDA (see Section 4.1). Each monolingual codebook that contains Gaussians after the LDA is approximately two megabytes. However, each language has a different LDA, therefore it is not possible to add a Gaussian from one codebook to another codebook. The three options are

- to store the Gaussians before the LDA as well on the embedded system

- to undo the LDA transformations with inverse LDA matrices as shown in Section 4.6.3

- to save each codebook after each LDA

The first option will produce the same results as the results in this thesis, but needs a couple of 100 megabytes of memory for 20 languages. The second option does not need additional memory, but will be worse and needs additional computational time. The third option produces good results, but also needs the most memory. Yet, for 10 languages the third option with about 200 megabyte might be acceptable.

The previous discussions showed that systems with up to 10 languages are possible with an acceptable runtime for the creation of MWCs. In fact, all that is to do is to load the right list, and append the desired number of Gaussians to the current codebook. This approach will require approximately 200 megabytes of memory. Of course, to precompute all the lists also takes time, but is possible in a couple of days on a current computer grid.

Yet, for more than 10 languages, the exponential dependencies outrun the engineering capabilities to precompute and store the necessary information. A possible idea for the determination which Gaussian to add is the following. Instead of computing a list for each language combination, only one list is compiled for each main language. This list contains in descending order of distance the Gaussians from all other languages. In addition to the distance, the list also saves from which language the Gaussian originated. If now an MWC has to be created, basically the list is traversed from the top and each Gaussian that belongs to one of the languages that should be supported will be added. However, again a trick has to applied to avoid to addition of two very similar Gaussians. The approach is to compare each addition candidate to the Gaussians that have already been added and skip it if it is too similar. To put the Gaussian in the right space, basically the same options as mentioned before are available.

Another possibility would be to have at most two additional languages that affect the MWC. This is a reasonable assumption, and will lead to only about 4000 lists ($\approx n \cdot \binom{20}{3}$) if the languages are chosen from a pool of 20 languages. The selection of languages can as always be based on the two most prominent languages in the music collection of a user, or on the geographic location of the user. It is important to note that the projection algorithm can still map all HMMs of all languages to this codebook, but only two will have improved coverage due to the MWC algorithm.

The list of possible enhancements could easily be extended. Examples are to consider only diagonal covariances for some parts of the calculation, to store already only diagonal covariances and so on. However, the most important concepts have been mentioned, and it became clear that an execution for up to 10 languages should be possible on an embedded system. Finally, it is also quite predictable that embedded systems will continue to become more powerful, and in a couple of years some options might be available that are currently not feasible. Especially when a connected car that is always online becomes true, much more options will be available.

6.4.4 Summary

This section evaluated the performance of a combination of the otfMHMM and the MWC algorithm. All figures from this section illustrated the benefits of this combination and approved that the otfMHMM gets better when the mismatch at the Gaussian level is reduced. For the general trends it became clear that Projection 7 is always the projection of choice, no matter if for native or non-native speech or if the algorithm is combined with MWC or not.

Another outcome from this section is that there are still problems that stem from the combinatoric explosion of possible systems. Section 6.4.3 has discussed this issue in detail. The general problem is that there are many lists that have to be precomputed. This section came to the conclusion that this problem is manageable if restrictions are accepted. Possible restrictions are to allow only 10 languages altogether, or to consider only MWCs that are influenced by at most two additional languages. Ultimately a solution can only be chosen for a specific embedded system.

It is also important to compare the results obtained in this section with the goals of this thesis. For easier reference, the itemization of issues of the previous Harman Becker multilingual speech recognition system from Section 1.2 is repeated here.

- Reduced performance on additional languages

- The training effort increased with the number of languages squared

- There were many more systems that had to be maintained

- The system design was rather inflexible, meaning that the recognizer could not adapt to the languages that are currently needed

Comparing these issues with the attributes of the scalable architecture depicted in Table 6.9 convincingly states that major issues are resolved with the new system. Apart from these technical aspects there are two further conclusions that can be

	Languages	Effort	Performance	Maintenance
Monolingual Codebook (Baseline)	Can recognize all language combinations	n^2 training effort	Suboptimal performance	Hard to maintain (high redundancy)
MWC	Can recognize some language combinations	$> 2^n$ training effort	Good performance	Very hard to maintain (highest redundancy)
otfMHMM	Can recognize all language combinations	Almost none	Worst Performance	Very easy (no redundancy)
MWC + otfMHMM	Can recognize all language combinations	Almost none	Scalable, can have best performance	Very easy (no redundancy)

Table 6.9: Comparison of how many languages can be recognized, the training effort, the performance and finally the maintenance effort.

drawn. First the additional work that is needed for the provision of multilingual speech recognition has diminished with the new architecture. Therefore the new system is cheaper and thus commercially more attractive. Second, there are still issues that have to be considered when this architecture is put into practice, but different solutions have been proposed.

With this section, the experiments that deal with the efficient and practical realization of multilingual speech recognition on embedded systems are finished. The next and final experimental section analyzes the algorithms that were proposed especially for the improved recognition of non-native accented speech.

6.5   Adaptation

6.5.1   Accent Detection and Language Identification through Codebook Share Rates

Before non-native accent dependent acoustic models can be created with adaptation methods it must be known which accent the user has. Another interesting question is to determine how strong the accent of the current speaker is. Actually, in the scenario of this thesis these questions are less relevant as this information can be determined from the language of the user interface and the language of the music title or origin of the navigation destination. For example, when a song has a French title and the user has set his user interface to German the song title is very likely uttered with German accent.

Despite the fact that it is not really necessary to extract this information from the actual speech signal in the setting of this thesis, this section shortly analyzes whether it is possible to do that just through the percentage of codebook use. In order to do that the codebooks from five languages where put into one large codebook. For each speech frame the 10 most likely Gaussians are collected.

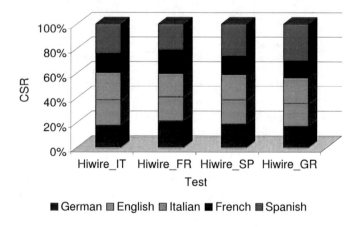

Figure 6.18: Accent detection through codebook share rate

Figure 6.18 depicts the percentage how often a Gaussian from one of the codebooks was among the best Gaussians for the Hiwire test sets. The hypothesis was that it might be possible to see a correlation, for example that the Italian codebook is dominating for the Italian accented Hiwire test. However, there are no such trends visible on in the graph. Thus these share rates of codebooks can probably not be used for accent detection.

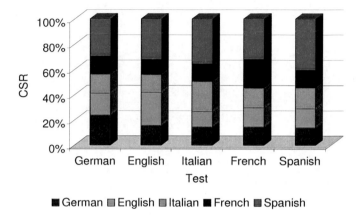

Figure 6.19: Language detection through codebook share rate

Another possible experiment was to test if a least native languages can be separated with the codebook share rate. This test was executed on the first block of the Speecon data (9 speakers for each language, roughly 3-4 hours of speech). Figure 6.19 presents the results. This time there is at least some relation, the codebook share rate is always highest for the corresponding language. For example, the highest share rate for the German codebook is achieved on the German test. The same is true for the other languages. However, the probably more direct observation is that the Spanish codebook always achieves the highest codebook share rate for all tests. Due to this fact, it is also questionable if the previously recognized relation can reliably be used to determine the language of a speech utterance. This is again another evidence that Spanish codebooks have different attributes than codebooks from other languages.

6.5.2 Durational Modeling

This section reports results on increasing the self-loop probabilities of HMMs for non-native speech in order to account for reduced speed of the speaker. It is the first of the algorithms presented in this thesis that focuses solely on improved modeling of non-native speech. This algorithm is also quite ambitious as it tries to improve the modeling without considering any special non-native data. It was shown in the

literature review (see Section 3.4.2) of this thesis that there are only few algorithms
that can report improvements for this most difficult scenario.

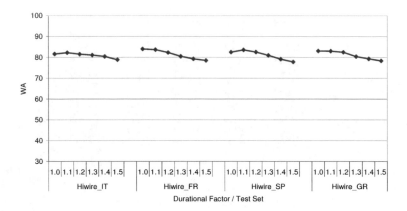

Figure 6.20: Effects of increasing the loop probabilities in HMMs for non-native
speech

Figure 6.20 depicts the results for an English classifier with an English codebook.
The x-axis labels indicate the factor with which the self loop probabilities were modified. The transition probability was set to one minus the loop probability to ensure
a sum of one. The picture depicts that there are no big improvements. A close
look shows small improvements for the Spanish and Italian accent, however both
improvements are insignificant (description of significance test in Appendix B).

6.5.3   Frequency Band Weight Adaptation

Frequency Band Weight Adaptation (FBWA) is the second algorithm from this thesis that tries to improve non-native speech recognition with no special non-native
adaptation data. Thus it is like the durational modeling (Section 6.5.2) algorithm
very ambitious. While the durational modeling algorithm has focused on the fact
that non-native speakers speak slower, this algorithm tries to utilize the fact that
non-native speakers vary more for certain frequencies (see Section 4.6.3). The FBWA
algorithm tries to utilize this by emphasizing or reducing the influence of frequency
bands. The frequency bands that can be modified are defined by the available MEL
bands of the recognizer (see Appendix C).

The results in this section are actually all only from the development sets of the
Hiwire data. This is because the original goal was to

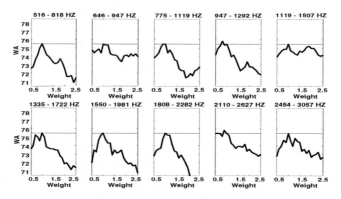

Figure 6.21: Effects of modifying the influence of mid-range frequency bands for native English speech

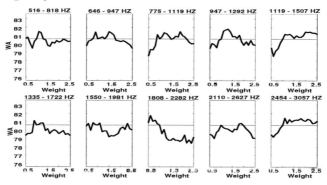

Figure 6.22: Effects of modifying frequency bands for Spanish accented English

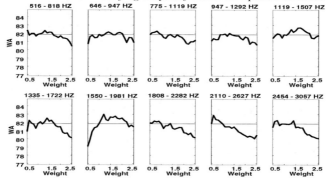

Figure 6.23: Effects of modifying frequency bands for Greek accented English

The first figures in this section report results where only one frequency band weight at a time is modified. These weights are the g_i as defined in Section 4.6.3. Each g_i) is individually varied between 0.5 and 2.5, while all other weights are kept fixed. Figure 6.21 illustrates the performance of 10 different frequency bands for the native English city test. The values of the corresponding frequency band weight are indicated on the x-axis. The horizontal line represents the baseline performance. As expected, the native models were optimized for native speech and every modification leads to clear drops in performance.

Figure 6.22 and Figure 6.23 show the same graphs for Spanish and Greek accented speech for the same 10 frequency bands. There is a significant difference to the behavior of the native speech test, in many cases the baseline is outperformed by the modifications. For example, for Spanish modifications from 700 to 1500 Hz help, and for Greek modifications in the range between 1100 and 2000Hz help. However, there is no clear correspondence between the Spanish and the Greek performance. One reason for this could be that changing one frequency band at a time is a too fine grained form of modification.

Therefore another set of experiments was performed, this time multiple frequency bands at once are adjusted. To reduce the number of possible combinations, the altogether 18 frequency bands were put in three groups; low, middle and high frequencies. Each of these groups contained 6 individual frequency bands. Each of the weights was varied between 0.6 and 1.4 in 0.2 steps. Figure 6.24, Figure 6.25 and Figure 6.26 depict the results of the best weight settings for the Spanish and the Greek Hiwire test.

Each individual diagram shows the performance for one fixed weight of the six high frequency bands. The weights for the middle and lower frequency bands are indicated below the x-axis of each diagram. As these modifications have a stronger impact than before, too large weight settings lead to decreased performance. For the Spanish Hiwire test some improvements are achieved with an increase of the influence of high frequencies. However, for the same weight settings, no improvements for Greek were achieved. Thus, it seems that improvements can only be accomplished with fine tuning for every accent. As this thesis tries to find methods that work without such fine tuning for every accent, no further experiments are made.

6.5.4   Model Merging

Model or State Merging is the third algorithm in this thesis that focuses on the improvement on non-native speech without additional non-native development data. In a first set of experiments the original setup in which model merging is proposed is

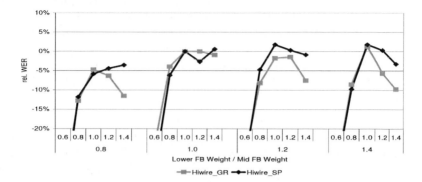

Figure 6.24: FBWA on Spanish and Greek accented English. The weight of the six high frequency bands is fixed to 1.0 in this diagram.

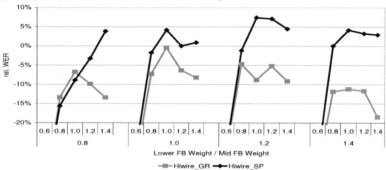

Figure 6.25: FBWA on Spanish and Greek accented English. The weight of the six high frequency bands is fixed to 1.2 in this diagram.

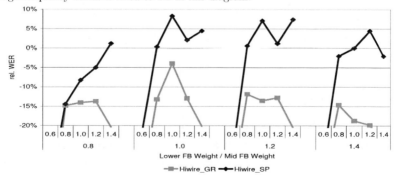

Figure 6.26: FBWA on Spanish and Greek accented English. The weight of the six high frequency bands is fixed to 1.4 in this diagram.

simulated as well as possible. This means that English HMM models that are trained
on an English codebook are modified. Figure 6.28, Figure 6.29 and Figure 6.27 depict
the performance for the French, Spanish and Italian Hiwire test. State merging refers
to tests where single states have been merged, and model merging refers to tests in
which HMM models were mapped and all three states of these models have been
merged together.

An analysis of one line of bars shows that both the Model and the State Merging
can improve over the baseline (the leftmost bars). On the Spanish Hiwire test the
performance increases from 82.5% WA to 85.4% WA for a Model Merging weight of
0.2. Performance improvements are also observed for the two other tests. On the
Italian Hiwire test from 81.6% to 83.8% WA and on the French Hiwire test from
83.9% to 85.3%. For weights between 0.2 and 0.5 the WA is increased on all three
tests.

Regarding the comparison between the state and the model based merging, it is
hard to make a decision based on these results. Therefore, this decision is delayed
after the next set of experiments that directly evaluates the benefits of Model Merging
for HMM models that use codebooks from the native language of the speakers. Only
the application of these codebooks already gave improvements for non-native speech,
as shown in Section 6.2.5. Thus the question is if Model Merging can also improve
this higher baseline.

Figure 6.31, Figure 6.32 and Figure 6.30 depict the behavior on the three test
sets. This time, as said before, the baseline is higher. The Spanish baseline is 86.6%,
the French baseline 86.0% and the Italian baseline 86.2%. The figures illustrate that
neither model merging nor state merging can improve beyond the increased baseline.

The reason for this is probably that both the application of Gaussians from the
native language of the speakers and model merging shift pronunciations that are
learned from native English speech in direction to non-native accented English. The
results demonstrate that these benefits are not additive.

6.5.5   HMM Adaptation

This thesis has evaluated many different algorithms in order to avoid the use of special
non-native development data, as this data is expensive. However, it is also interesting
to see what performance can be achieved with such additional data. Therefore this
section presents results after the English HMM models have been retrained with
non-native development data. Note that for consistency with the rest of this thesis,
all diagrams contain results from the benchmark system (the monolingual English

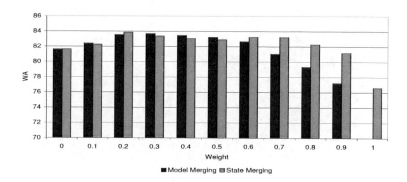

Figure 6.27: State and Model Merging on the Italian Hiwire test (US_1024 C1)

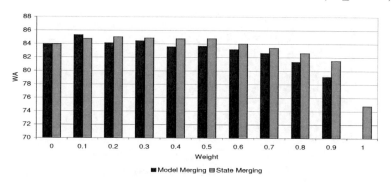

Figure 6.28: State and Model Merging on the French Hiwire test (US_1024 C1)

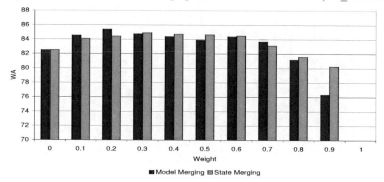

Figure 6.29: State and Model Merging on the Spanish Hiwire test (US_1024 C1)

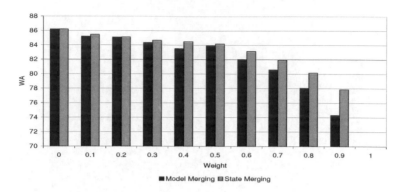

Figure 6.30: State and Model Merging on the Italian Hiwire test (IT_1024 C1)

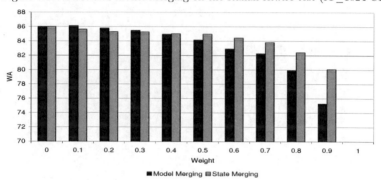

Figure 6.31: State and Model Merging on the French Hiwire test (FR_1024 C1)

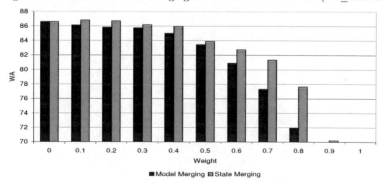

Figure 6.32: State and Model Merging on the Spanish Hiwire test (SP_1024 C1)

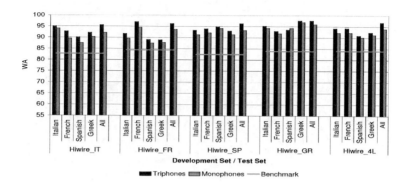

Figure 6.33: Retraining and testing on Hiwire

system). However, in this section this system really has to be regarded as baseline, as the adaptation with additional data should get better.

Figure 6.33 illustrates the benefits from a retraining on the Hiwire development data. The figure also shows results for cross accent performance, as system have been trained on one accent and are tested on another. The last development set "All" refers to a retraining on all four development sets from Hiwire. Similarly, the last test Hiwire_4L indicates the average performance on all four Hiwire accents.

As expected, the improvements are much higher than any of the previous results. For example, after retraining on Greek and testing on Greek 97.6% WA are achieved, and for French a 97.0% WA was achieved. The figure demonstrates that retraining on other accents can help, as for example retraining on Italian and testing on Greek still leads to 95.2% WA, much higher than the benchmark performance of 83.9% WA on the Greek test set. The results also show that the triphone system outperforms a monophone system.

However, these results, although comparable to many results in the literature, are probably somewhat optimistic. The reasons for this are that the development data has exactly the same channel conditions as the test and that the speakers of the development set and the test set are the same. Thus these improvements also include speaker specific adaptation benefits. To eliminate both additional effects, the systems that were retrained on the Hiwire development data are tested on test sets from the ISLE corpus. The results are depicted in Figure 6.34.

The results are disappointing, as the performance of both monophone and triphone systems is below the benchmark system. This could indicate that the previous benefits were only due to some of the other effects, and not due to adaptation to

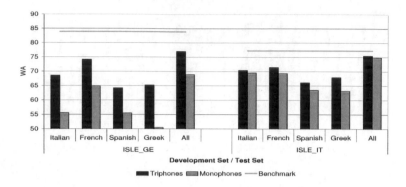

Figure 6.34: Retraining on Hiwire and testing on ISLE

non-native speech. However, it is also true the Hiwire database contains only a limited vocabulary, and thus it could have happened that some monophones were more or less adapted to a special triphone, as this occurred so frequently in the Hiwire adaptation data.

These issues are analyzed in Figure 6.35. The figure shows that many of the triphones that occur in the ISLE test data do not occur in the Hiwire development set. In fact, there are more triphones in the ISLE that are not covered by the development set than triphones that are covered. The graphs also indicate that the ISLE corpus, that was designed to be a phonetically rich corpus contains much more triphones than the Hiwire corpus. Thus the last experiment in this evaluates if an adaptation in the other direction, meaning an adaptation on ISLE and testing on Hiwire yields benefits.

Figure 6.36 shows that this really is better than an adaptation on the unbalanced Hiwire data. The benchmark system is outperformed in all cases by the monophone recognition systems. However, the triphone acoustic model is still worse, probably due to insufficient training data for each triphone. Thus this section has shown that well-adapted triphones outperform monophones (Figure 6.33), but monophone acoustic models are the better choice if the development data is not sufficient (Figure 6.36). It became also clear that an adaptation with unbalanced development data can reduce the performance significantly. The diploma thesis of [Lang 09a] explains the results in further detail.

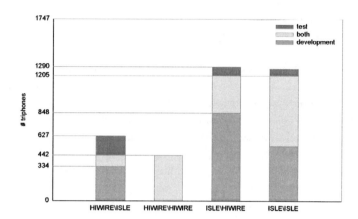

Figure 6.35: Triphone coverage of development and test sets. The x-axis indicates the applied development data D and the test T by D\T.

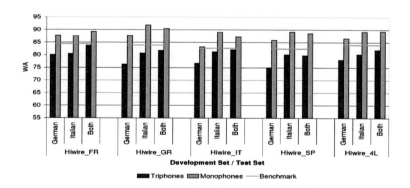

Figure 6.36: Retraining on ISLE and testing on Hiwire

6.5.6 Summary

This section has evaluated different algorithms for HMM adaptation to non-native speech. At first, it was analyzed if accents or languages can be identified through codebook share rates. The answer was no, but this is not a problem in the context of this thesis, as the languages and accents can be determined from the interface of the graphical user interface and the current task that is executed by the user.

The next three algorithms dealt with the difficult scenario of improving non-native recognition without any additional data. The first algorithm was durational modeling. It is a quite simple algorithm that modified the self loop and transition probabilities within HMMs. The goal of this algorithm was to account for a slower speaking rate of non-native speakers, but no improvements were observed. The second algorithm had a similar motivation, this time the goal was to account for the fact that non-native speakers differ more in certain frequency ranges and less in others. The results showed small improvements, but there was no clear tendency for different accents, thus this technique is also not suitable for commercial application. Finally, Model Merging (originally proposed by [Witt 99b]) was reevaluated. Some changes had to be made to the algorithm in order to work with semi-continuous HMMs. The results verified that Model Merging can also help in semi-continuous systems, but a combination with a codebook of the native language of the speakers showed no additional improvements.

Finally, the more common adaptation with development data was analyzed. As expected, this yielded by far the best recognition rates, but is quite unrealistic for an application in large scale. In contrast to previous work, this section also evaluated across databases to eliminate influences of speaker and channel adaptation. This changed the results significantly. The conclusions from this section are that triphones are better than monophones if sufficient adaptation data is available, that similar accents help to improve non-native recognition and that monophones are better with scarce adaptation data.

Chapter 7

Outlook

This thesis has evaluated the literature in the area of multilingual speech recognition and proposed a new, scalable architecture. The new architecture has many advantages, but there is still room for improvement. One major issue that has to be solved is how it can really be implemented on an embedded system. Section 6.4.3 showed that the problem here is to generate the MWC.

The same section also proposed many engineering approaches to allow the MWC generation, but each of them has a disadvantage. Some of them require expensive precomputations, some of them require relatively large amounts of hard disk memory and some of them have a negative impact on the recognition performance. The most promising alternatives are probably to allow only a limited number of languages to have influence on the codebook generation or to generate a large list that contains in sorted order the distances to all other languages.

As the time goes by, even completely new options may arise. A key initiative of today is to make a connected car that has always or almost always access to the Internet a reality. In such an environment new alternatives are possible. For example, for a given main language all required files could be downloaded to the system, thus reducing the hard disk requirements on the embedded system. This would still ensure that the in-car system can operate independently after the download has finished.

Another area for improvement is the performance on non-native speech that still suffers from the mismatched training data with native speech. For example, the last section in Chapter 6 showed that the performance of adaptation with non-native development data is still unmatched. However, it is not feasible to collect all possible accents in a true multilingual scenario to perform all trainings with perfectly well matched training data.

As a matter of fact, to achieve maximum performance it would probably be necessary to record each accent multiple times, as there are strongly accented speakers, medium accented and almost not accented speakers. This division in three levels is still a simplification, as a person's way of speaking is to some extend unique. The only solution that could really achieve an optimal performance is a speaker dependent system.

However, the known high recognition rates of 99% of speaker identification stem from clean speech tests [Camp 97] where initial training data was available. Speaker identification in a noisy environment and without initial training data poses still major problems [Reyn 95, Herb 10]. It is clear that potential users will not like a system that they have to train before they can use the system. In order to avoid this, the system needs to perform an unsupervised adaptation to the user of the system. Yet, this is difficult, as the user can change, and the system also needs to detect when a new user occurs.

These questions are explored in detail in [Herb 10], a PhD thesis that was performed in parallel to this thesis at HBAS. This thesis proposes a system that can answer these questions and thus allows an unsupervised adaptation to the users. Given the large improvements this thesis has seen with non-native development data, a combination could maybe close the gap between recognition rates on native and non-native speakers. With the work in this thesis, this might be possible without an increase of the required resources on the target system by creating the basic system on-the-fly and then increasing the performance through unsupervised speaker adaptation.

Chapter 8

Summary

This thesis has proposed a scalable architecture for multilingual speech recognition on embedded devices. At first it was motivated where and why multilingual speech recognition is necessary at the example of a tourist that is going on holiday with his car. From a technical point of view this poses two major problems for a speech operated car infotainment system. First, the user utters destinations from foreign countries with non-native accent. Second, the system has to offer the possibility to recognize names from many different languages, for example for spoken music selection.

Chapter 2 introduced the fundamentals of speech recognition. The main concept is the statistical framework that finds the most likely word sequence by combining the information from a language and an acoustic model for a given utterance. The acoustic model outputs for all models how likely it is that they produced the current feature vector. The system of this thesis uses HMMs for the modeling of the sequence of sounds and Gaussians that model the feature output probabilities for each single HMM state. More detailed, it is a semi-continuous system that has only one codebook for all HMM states of a language. To complete the components that typically influence a speech recognition system, the language model and dictionary were also shortly discussed. At the end of this section, the applied evaluation measure was introduced.

Chapter 3 analyzed the literature about multilingual and non-native speech recognition. Although there is a common notion what accent is, there is no single feature in a speech signal that represents this notion of accents. Instead, it is a combination of different signal attributes that lead to perceived accents of speakers. Four different theories about second language learners were described. While the initial theories tried to predict errors, the newest theory has resigned this goal, and only tries to explain errors. These explanations are both based on differences between the languages

131

as well as on attributes that solely depend on the language to be learned. Regarding multilingual ASR, one finding was that it is difficult to compare different work in this area, as each work deals with slightly different constraints. Another finding was that almost monolingual performance ASR can be achieved by a technique that combines an IPA based mapping with additional clustering at the density level. An important aspect for multilingual speech recognizers is their performance on non-native speech. A key issue here is that there are many accents, and it is infeasible to have appropriate data for all accents. Therefore the most desirable techniques should not require any non-native resources. The literature review found some solutions that relied only on information from the native language of the speakers. Other techniques rely on human expertise or on some additional adaptation data for each new speaker. The greatest improvements were unsurprisingly reported with non-native development data.

Chapter 4 described the algorithms that are tested in this thesis. All of them are based on findings from the literature review, but only the HMM adaptation is a standard algorithm that was used before. It is a common idea to think of monolingual systems as upper bound for the performance of the proposed multilingual system. In the rest of this thesis these systems were therefore called benchmark systems. The baseline system is a system that retrains HMMs of all languages on a given codebook to allow the recognition of all languages with this codebook. The Multilingual Weighted Codebook algorithm was then proposed to optimize a single codebook for the recognition of all additional languages. Three different distance measures have been suggested for the determination of the similarity of single Gaussians. As a solution to the exponentially increased training effort that is required for systems that rely on MWCs, projections between Gaussian spaces were presented. At first mathematical optimal projections based on the L2 distance between Gaussian mixture models were derived. The projections differ in the constraints that they keep. In addition, approximated projections with less computational effort were proposed. This section also showed that the two previous algorithms can be combined to a scalable architecture that allows to tailor an individual system for each user of the system. Finally five algorithms for the additional adaptation of systems to non-native speech are introduced.

Chapter 5 discussed the data that was available for non-native speech recognition at the time this thesis was written. This chapter also motivated why it is difficult to have appropriate data for experiments on non-native speech recognition and gives an overview of non-native speech databases. The most promising databases were reviewed in detail for their applicability for this thesis. The second part of this chapter describes the training, development and test sets. Training data for five languages was used from the Speecon database. There were six different development sets, two from ISLE and four from Hiwire. The different sets are necessary to adapt to different accents. The last section defines 14 different test sets, seven native and seven non-native tests. The test sets cover five native languages and eight accents.

Chapter 6 evaluated the algorithms that were proposed before. A first set of experiments indicated that triphones can perform up to 16% WER better than monophones on non-native speech if they are trained with enough data. The experiments with MWCs showed that only 10% additional Gaussians can already give more than 60% of the improvement from adding all Gaussians on native speech. The extension to five languages showed that the observed improvements are completely independent of the considered languages. It also became clear that the application of the native codebook of the speakers gives significant improvements in the range of 25% relative WER over the benchmark system for accented English. The MWCs kept this improvement, and performed up to 30% relative WER better on native speech than the baseline system. This chapter also assessed the projections between Gaussian spaces. The approximated projections needed much less time than the mathematically motivated projections and achieved comparable WER rates. The evaluation of speech recognition performance was then extended to more languages and to non-native accents. The projections alone need only one fiftythousandth of the time of a Baum-Welch retraining and make the creation of new systems as easy as a snap of fingers. For native speech, the scalable architecture outperformed the baseline system by up to 25% relative WER. For non-native speech, the scalable architecture came close to the performance of the benchmark systems, but these benchmark systems are unfeasible on an embedded system, and the scalabale architecture is feasible. In summary, the scalable architecture is cheaper and there is almost no additional maintenance effort. Furthermore it supports any combination of languages which increases the user friendliness of speech based systems. With all these advantages the proposed system should be considered as a standard for speech recognition in the future. The rest of this chapter evaluated some algorithms that could lead to further improved recognition on non-native accented speech. The modeling of slower speaking rates reported improvements of up to 8% relative WER. The Frequency Band Weight Adaptation did also improve by roughly 8% relative WER for Spanish accented English. Model Merging achieved improvements of up to 17% relative WER over the benchmark system. Finally, systems were retrained with development data. This gave tremendous improvements and reduced for example the WER on French accented English by 80% relative and by 85.1% relative WER on Greek accented English.

Chapter 7 discussed the possibilities for future work. One open task is to really implement the whole architecture on an embedded system and another task to combine the introduced work with unsupervised speaker adaptation algorithms to improve the recognition performance on non-native speech.

The experiments in this thesis have lead to new insights for multilingual and non-native ASR. They showed that a codebook in a semi-continuous system is of vital importance for the enhanced recognition of multilingual tasks. Furthermore, they showed that it can help for the recognition of non-native speech to use mismatching codebooks and HMM training data. Finally, a combination of algorithms proposed in this thesis lead to a scalable architecture that allows the creation of practical multilingual ASR systems for any combination of languages within almost no time.

Appendix A

Own Publications

All papers can be accessed at http://www.segv.de/~mraab/.

1. M. Raab. *Co-operative learning in mathematics - An attempt to foster asynchronous co-operation via email in higher education.* Studienarbeit, Institut für Algorithmen und Kognitive Systeme, Universität Karlsruhe, Karlsruhe, Germany, 2004

2. S. Stueker, C. Fuegen, R. Hsiao, S. Ikbal, Q. Jin, F. Kraft, M. Paulik, M. Raab, Y. Tam, and M.Woelfel. "The ISL TC-STAR spring 2006 ASR evaluation systems". In: *Proc. of the TC-STAR Workshop on Speech-to-Speech Translation*, Barcelona, Spain, 2006

3. M. Raab. *Language modeling for machine translation.* Diplomarbeit, Institut für Theoretische Informatik, Universität Karlsruhe, Karlsruhe, Germany, 2006

4. M. Raab, R. Gruhn, and E. Nöth. "Non-native speech databases". In: *Proc. ASRU*, pp. 413–418, Kyoto, Japan, 2007

5. M. Raab. *Language modeling for machine translation.* Vdm Verlag, Saarbruecken, Germany, 2007

6. M. Raab. "Non-native speech databases". 2008.
   http://en.wikipedia.org/wiki/Non-native_speech_databases

7. M. Raab, R. Gruhn, and E. Nöth. "Multilingual weighted codebooks". In: *Proc. ICASSP*, pp. 4257–4260, Las Vegas, USA, 2008

8. M. Raab, R. Gruhn, and E. Nöth. "Codebook design for speech guided car infotainment systems". In: *Proc. PIT*, pp. 44–51, Kloster Irsee, Germany, 2008

9. M. Raab, T. Herbig, R. Brückner, R. Gruhn, and E. Nöth. "Adaptation of frequency band influence for non-native speech recognition". In: *Proc. ESSV*, pp. 149–156, Frankfurt, Germany, 2008

10. M. Raab, R. Gruhn, and E. Nöth. "Multilingual weighted codebooks for non-native speech recognition". In: *Proc. TSD*, pp. 485–492, Brno, Czech Republic, 2008

11. M. Raab, O. Schreiner, T. Herbig, R. Gruhn, and E. Nöth. "Optimal projections between Gaussian mixture feature spaces for multilingual speech recognition". In: *Proc. DAGA*, pp. 411–414, Rotterdam, Netherlands, 2009

12. H. Lang, M. Raab, R. Gruhn, and W. Minker. "Comparing acoustic model adaption methods for non-native speech recognition". In: *Proc. DAGA*, pp. 87–90, Rotterdam, Netherlands, 2009

13. M. Raab, G. Aradilla, R. Gruhn, and E. Nöth. "Online generation of acoustic models for multilingual speech recognition". In: *Proc. Interspeech*, pp. 2999–3002, Brighton, UK, 2009

14. M. Raab, R. Gruhn, and E. Nöth. "Multilingual speech interfaces for resource-constrained dialog systems". In: *Proc. IWSDS*, Kloster Irsee, Germany, 2009

Appendix B

Significance Test

A frequent problem in speech recognition is to compare different recognizers using different settings for algorithms and/or the training of the recognizers. The question to answer is whether one of the systems is better than the other, or if the different performance can be regarded as likely to be caused by accident.

A significance test can be used to judge the probability that one recognizer is better than the other. It is important to know, and often confused, that a significance test is not generating the likelihood that one recognizer is better than the other. Rather it states that the likelihood that the assumption that recognizer A is better than recognizer B is wrong is less than the level of significance.

In general, in order to test significance it is necessary to make an **assumption** of the probability distribution which has generated the number of observed samples. Deciding which probability function to use is difficult and not straightforward. In many cases, due to the rather simple evaluation common assumptions are that the samples are generated by a Gaussian distribution or by a Bernoulli distribution.

For a significance test on speech recognizers the Bernoulli assumption is most common. In literature this test is referred to as signed Matched Pair Test [Huan 01]. To evaluate the significance **S**, one has to collect all **n** differences of the two recognizers A and B on the same test set. On these n differences, A was **k** times correct and B was n-k times correct. The a priori probability that A is better than B is **p** is 0.5.

Then the significance S that recognizer A is better than B is

$$S(k, n, p) = 1 - \sum_{j=k}^{n} \binom{n}{j} p^k (1 - p)^{n-j}$$

The lower the significance, the higher the likelihood that A is better than B (to be exact, the sentence has to be 'the lower the significance, the likelihood that the assumption that A is better than B is wrong is less than the level of significance').

In general, a recognizer A is said to be weak significant if S < 0.1, significant if S < 0.05 and highly significant if S < 0.01.

Appendix C

Mel Bands

Section 4.6.3 has described how the influence of frequency bands can be adjusted. For the results, it is interesting to relate the different bands to their actual frequency range. In this thesis the experiments are conducted on 11 kHz data. For such a sampling rate, a 256 discrete Fourier transformation is used on which 18 MEL bands are calculated. The frequency range of each Mel band is given in Table C.1.

MEL band	Start	End
1	129.2 Hz	387.6 Hz
2	215.3 Hz	473.7 Hz
3	301.5 Hz	602.9 Hz
4	430.7 Hz	689.1 Hz
5	516.8 Hz	818.3 Hz
6	646.0 Hz	947.5 Hz
7	775.2 Hz	1119.7 Hz
8	947.5 Hz	1292.0 Hz
9	1119.7 Hz	1507.3 Hz
10	1335.1 Hz	1722.7 Hz
11	1550.4 Hz	1981.1 Hz
12	1808.8 Hz	2282.5 Hz
13	2110.3 Hz	2627.1 Hz
14	2454.8 Hz	3057.7 Hz
15	2885.4 Hz	3574.5 Hz
16	3402.2 Hz	4220.5 Hz
17	4048.2 Hz	5038.8 Hz
18	4866.5 Hz	5512.5 Hz

Table C.1: MEL bands for 11025 recognizer

List of Figures

List of Tables

Bibliography

[Amda 00] I. Amdal, F. Korkmazskiy, and A. C. Surendran. "Joint pronunciation modelling of non-native speakers using data-driven methods". In: *Proc. Interspeech*, pp. 622–625, Beijing, China, 2000.

[AMI 07] AMI Project. "Augmented multi-party interaction meeting corpus". 2007. http://corpus.amiproject.org/.

[Ande 93] O. Andersen, P. Dalsgaard, and W. Barry. "Data driven identification of poly- and mono-phonemes for four European languages". In: *Proc. Eurospeech*, pp. 759–762, Berlin, Germany, 1993.

[Arsl 96] L. M. Arslan. *Foreign accent classification in American English*. PhD thesis, Duke University, Durham, USA, 1996.

[Arsl 97] L. M. Arslan and J. H. Hansen. "Frequency characteristics of foreign accented speech". In: *Proc. ICASSP*, pp. 1123–1126, Munich, Germany, 1997.

[Bart 06] K. Bartkova and D. Jouvet. "Using multilingual units for improved modeling of pronunciation variants". In: *Proc. ICASSP*, pp. 1037–1040, Toulouse, France, 2006.

[Baus 79] K. R. Bausch and G. Kasper. "Der Zweitsprachenerwerb: Möglichkeiten und Grenzen der großen Hypothesen". *Linguistische Berichte*, pp. 3–35, 1979.

[Bena 99] L. Benarousse, E. Geoffrois, J. Grieco, R. Series, H. Steeneken, H. Stumpf, C. Swail, and D. Thiel. "The NATO native and non-native (N4) speech corpus". In: *Proc. of the MIST workshop (ESCA-NATO)*, pp. 1–3, Leusden, The Netherlands, Sep 1999.

[Bieh 90] M. Biehl, J. K. Anlauf, and W. Kinzel. "Perceptron Learning by Constrained Optimization: the AdaTron algorithm". In: *Proc. ASI Summer Workshop Neurodynamics*, Clausthal, Germany, 1990.

[Bisa 04] M. Bisani and H. Ney. "Bootstrap estimates for confidence intervals in ASR performance evaluation". In: *Proc. ICASSP*, pp. 409–412, Montreal, Canada, 2004.

[Bode 07] N. Bodenstab and M. Fanty. "Multi-pass pronunciation adaptation". In: *Proc. ICASSP*, pp. 865–868, Honolulu, Hawaii, 2007.

[Bona 97] P. Bonaventura, F. Gallocchio, and G. Micca. "Multilingual speech recognition for flexible vocabularies". In: *Proc. Eurospeech*, pp. 355–358, Rhodes, Greece, 1997.

[Bous 05]   G. Bouselmi, D. Fohr, I. Illina, and J. P. Haton. "Fully automated non-native speech recognition using confusion-based acoustic model integration". In: *Proc. Interspeech*, pp. 1369–1372, Lisbon, Portugal, 2005.

[Bous 06a]   G. Bouselmi, D. Fohr, I. Illina, and J. P. Haton. "Fully automated non-native speech recognition using confusion-based acoustic model integration and graphemic constraints". In: *Proc. ICASSP*, pp. 345–348, Toulouse, France, 2006.

[Bous 06b]   G. Bouselmi, D. Fohr, I. Illina, and J. P. Haton. "Multilingual non-native speech recognition using confusion-based acoustic model modicication and graphemic constraints". In: *Proc. Interspeech*, pp. 109–112, Pittsburgh, USA, 2006.

[Bous 07]   G. Bouselmi, D. Fohr, and I. Illina. "Combined acoustic and pronunciation modeling for non-native speech recognition". In: *Proc. Interspeech*, pp. 1449–1552, Antwerp, Belgium, 2007.

[Bous 08]   G. Bouselmi. *Reconnaissance automatique de la parole non native*. PhD thesis, LORIA-CNRS & INRIA Nancy, Nancy, France, 2008.

[Boyd 04]   S. Boyd and L. Vandenberghe. *Convex Optimization*. Cambridge University Press, 2004.

[Byrn 98]   W. Byrne, E. Knodt, S. Khudanpur, and J. Bernstein. "Is automatic speech recognition ready for non-native speech? A data-collection effort and initial experiments in modeling conversational Hispanic English". In: *STiLL*, pp. 37–40, Marholmen, Sweden, 1998.

[Camp 97]   J. P. Campbell. "Speaker recognition: a tutorial". In: *Proc. of the IEEE, Vol. 85, no. 9*, pp. 1437–1462, 1997.

[Ceti 07]   Ö. Cetin, M. Magimai-Doss, K. Livescu, A. Kantor, S. King, C. Bartels, and J. Frankel. "Monolingual and crosslingual comparison of tandem features derived from articulatory and phone MLPS". In: *Proc. ASRU*, pp. 36–41, Kyoto, Japan, 2007.

[Chom 65]   N. Chomsky. *Aspects of the theory of syntax*. MIT Press, Cambridge, USA, 1965.

[Cier 04]   C. Cieri, D. Miller, and K. Walker. "The Fisher corpus: a resource for the next generations of speech-to-text". In: *Proc. LREC*, pp. 69–71, Lisbon, Portugal, 2004.

[Cord 67]   S. P. Corder. "The significance of learners errors". *International Review of Applied Linguistics*, pp. 161–170, 1967.

[Dals 92]   P. Dalsgaard and O. Andersen. "Identification of mono- and polyphonemes using acoustic-phonetic features derived by a self-organising neural network". In: *Proc. ICSLP*, pp. 547–550, Banff, Canada, 1992.

[Dals 98]   P. Dalsgaard, O. Andersen, and W. Barry. "Cross-language merged speech units and their descriptive phonetic correlates". In: *Proc. ICSLP*, p. no pagination, Sydney, Australia, 1998.

[Falk 95]   M. Falkhausen, H. Reininger, and D. Wolf. "Calculation of distance measures between Hidden Markov Models". In: *Proc. Eurospeech*, pp. 1487–1490, Madrid, Spain, 1995.

[Fede]   Federal Aviation Administration. "Controller pilot datalink communications (CPDLC)". http://tf.tc.faa.gov/capabilities/cpdlc.htm.

[Fisc 03]   V. Fischer, E. Janke, and S. Kunzmann. "Recent progress in the decoding of non-native speech with multilingual acoustic models". In: *Proc. Interspeech*, pp. 3105–3108, Geneva, Switzerland, 2003.

[Fisc 97]   J. Fiscus. "A post processing system to yield reduced word error rates: Recognizer Output Voting Error Reduction (ROVER)". In: *Proc. ASRU*, pp. 347–354, Santa Barbara, USA, 1997.

[Fitt 95]   S. Fitt. "The pronunciation of unfamiliar native and non-native town names". In: *Proc. Eurospeech*, pp. 2227–2230., Madrid, Spain, 1995.

[Frie 45]   C. Fries. *Teaching and learning English as a foreign language*. University of Michigan Press, Ann Arbor, USA, 1945.

[Furu 07]   S. Furui. "50 years of progress in speech recognition technology - Where we are, and where we should go". 2007. http://ewh.ieee.org/soc/sps/stc/News/NL0704/furui-icassp2007.pdf.

[Goro 01a] S. Goronzy, R. Kompe, and S. Rapp. "Generating non-native pronunciation variants for lexicon adaptation". In: *Proc. ITRW*, pp. 143–146, Sophia Antipolis, France, 2001.

[Goro 01b] S. Goronzy, M. Sahakyan, and W. Wokurek. "Is non-native pronunciation modeling necessary?". In: *Proc. Interspeech*, pp. 309–312, Aalborg, Denmark, 2001.

[Goro 02]   S. Goronzy. *Robust adaptation to non-native accents in automatic speech recognition*. Springer, 2002.

[Gruh 04a] R. Gruhn, T. Cincarek, and S. Nakamura. "A multi-accent non-native English database". In: *Proc. ASJ*, pp. 163–164, 2004.

[Gruh 04b] R. Gruhn, K. Markov, and S. Nakamura. "A statistical lexicon for non-native speech recognition". In: *Proc. Interspeech*, pp. 1497–1500, Jeju Island, Korea, 2004.

[Gruh 08]   R. Gruhn. *Statistical Pronunciation Modeling for Non-Native Speech Processing*. PhD thesis, University of Ulm, Ulm, Germany, 2008.

[Hack 07]   C. Hacker, T. Cincarek, A. Maier, A. Hessler, and E. Nöth. "Boosting of prosodic and pronunciation features to detect mispronunciations of non-native children". In: *Proc. ICASSP*, pp. 197–200, Honolulu, Hawaii, 2007.

[He 01]   X. He and Y. Zhao. "Model Complexity Optimization for Nonnative English Speakers". In: *Proc. Interspeech*, pp. 1461–1464, Aalborg, Denmark, 2001.

[Herb 10]   T. Herbig. *Self-Learning Speaker Identification System for Enhanced Speech Recognition in an Automotive Environment*. PhD thesis, University of Ulm, Ulm, Germany, to be published in 2010.

[Hers 07]   J. R. Hershey and P. A. Olsen. "Approximating the Kullback Leibler Divergence Between Gaussian Mixture Models". In: *Proc. ICASSP*, pp. 317–320, Honolulu, Hawaii, 2007.

150 *Bibliography*

[Heuv 06]   H. Heuvel, K. Choukri, C. Gollan, A. Moreno, and D. Mostefa. "TC-STAR: New language resources for ASR and SLT purposes". In: *Proc. LREC*, pp. 2570–2573, Genoa, Italy, 2006.

[Huan 01]   X. Huang, A. Acero, and H. Hon. *Spoken language processing: a guide to theory, algorithm and system development.* Prentice Hall, 2001.

[Huan 90]   X. Huang, K. F. Lee, and H. W. Hon. "On semi-continuous hidden Markov modeling". In: *Proc. ICASSP*, pp. 689–692, Albuquerque, USA, 1990.

[Impe 99]   B. Imperl and B. Horvat. "The clustering algorithm for the definition of multilingual set of context dependent speech models". In: *Proc. Eurospeech*, pp. 887–890, Budapest, Hungary, 1999.

[Iskr 02]   D. Iskra, B. Grosskopf, K. Marasek, H. van den Huevel, F. Diehl, and A. Kiessling. "Speecon - speech databases for consumer devices: database specification and validation". In: *Proc. LREC*, pp. 329–333, Las Palmas de Gran Canaria, Spain, 2002.

[Jens 07]   J. H. Jensen, D. P. W. Ellis, M. Christensen, and S. H. Jensen. "Evaluation of distance measures between Gaussian mixture models of MFCCs". In: *Proc. ISMIR*, pp. 107–108, Vienna, Austria, 2007.

[Jian 05]   B. Jian and B. C. Vemuri. "A robust algorithm for point set registration using mixture of Gaussians". In: *Proc. IEEE Int Conf Comput Vision*, pp. 1246–1251, Beijing, China, 2005.

[Juan 85]   B. H. Juang and L. R. Rabiner. "A probabilistic distance measure for Hidden Markov Models". *AT&T Technical Journal*, Vol. 64, No. 2, pp. 391–408, 1985.

[Jura 00]   D. Jurafsky and J. H. Martin. *Speech and Language Processing: An Introduction to Natural Language Processing, Computational Linguistics and Speech Recognition.* Prentice Hall, first Ed., 2000.

[Jura 94]   D. Jurafsky, C. Wooters, G. Tajchman, J. Segal, A. Stolcke, E. Fosler, and N. Morgan. "The Berkeley restaurant project". In: *Proc. ICSLP*, pp. 2139–2142, Yokohama, Japan, 1994.

[Kim 07]   M. Kim, Y. R. Oh, and H. K. Kim. "Non-native pronunciation variation modeling using an indirect data driven method". In: *Proc. ASRU*, pp. 231–236, Kyoto, Japan, 2007.

[Koeh 01]   J. Koehler. "Multilingual phone models for vocabulary-independent speech recognition tasks". *Speech Communication Journal*, Vol. 35, No. 1-2, pp. 21–30, 2001.

[Kuhn 51]   H. W. Kuhn and A. W. Tucker. "Nonlinear Programming". In: *Proc. of 2nd Berkeley Symposium*, pp. 481–492, Berkeley, USA, 1951.

[Kuhn 98]   R. Kuhn, P. Nguyen, J.-C. Junqua, L. Goldwasser, N. Niedzielski, S. Fincke, K. Field, and M. Contolini. "Eigenvoices for speaker adaptation". In: *Proc. ICSLP*, pp. 1771–1774, Sydney, Australia, 1998.

[Kull 51]   S. Kullback and R. Leibler. "On information and sufficiency". *Annals of Mathematical Statistics*, Vol. 22, No. 1, pp. 79–86, 1951.

[Lade 90]   P. Ladefoged. "The revised international phonetic Alphabet". *Language*, Vol. 66, No. 3, pp. 550–552, 1990.

[Lado 57]   R. Lado. *Linguistics across cultures: applied linguistics for language teachers*. University of Michigan Press, Ann Arbor, USA, 1957.

[Lame 94]   L. Lamel, F. Schiel, A. Fourcin, J. Mariani, and H. Tillmann. "The translanguage English database TED". In: *Proc. ICSLP*, pp. 1795–1798, Yokohama, Japan, Sep 1994.

[Land 07]   T. Lander. "CSLU: foreign accented English release 1.2". Tech. Rep., LDC, Philadelphia, USA, 2007.

[Lang 09a]   H. Lang. *Methods for the adaptation of acoustic models to non-native speakers*. Diplomarbeit, Institute of Information Technology, University Ulm, Ulm, Germany, 2009.

[Lang 09b]   H. Lang, M. Raab, R. Gruhn, and W. Minker. "Comparing acoustic model adaption methods for non-native speech recognition". In: *Proc. DAGA*, pp. 87–90, Rotterdam, Netherlands, 2009.

[LaRo 02]   A. LaRocca and R. Chouairi. "West Point Arabic speech corpus". Tech. Rep., LDC, Philadelphia, USA, 2002.

[LaRo 03]   A. LaRocca and C. Tomei. "West Point Russian speech corpus". Tech. Rep., LDC, Philadelphia, USA, 2003.

[Li 05]   M. Li. *Die finale F0-Kontur der Ja/Nein-Fragen des Deutschen*. Studienarbeit, Institut für maschinelle Spracherarbeitung, University Stuttgart, Ulm, Germany, 2005.

[Lin 08]   H. Lin, L. Deng, J. Droppo, D. Yu, and A. Acero. "Learning methods in multilingual speech recognition". In: *Proc. NIPS*, Vancouver, Canada, 2008.

[Lind 80]   Y. Linde, A. Buzo, and R. Gray. "An algorithm for vector quantization design". *IEEE Transactions on Communications*, Vol. 28, No. 1, pp. 84–95, 1980.

[List 81]   G. List. *Sprachpsychologie*. Kohlhammer, 1981.

[Live 99]   K. Livescu. *Analysis and modeling of non-native speech for automatic speech recognition*. Master's thesis, Department of Electrical Engineering and Computer Science, Massachusetts Institute of Technology, Cambridge, USA, 1999.

[Maha 36]   P. Mahalanobis. "On the generalised distance in statistics". In: *Proc. of the National Institute of Science of India 12*, pp. 49–55, 1936.

[Mak 96]   B. Mak and E. Barnard. "Phone clustering using the Bhattacharya distance". In: *Proc. ICSLP*, pp. 2005–2008, Philadelphia, USA, 1996.

[Menz 00]   W. Menzel, E. Atwell, P. Bonaventura, D. Herron, P. Howarth, R. Morton, and C. Souter. "The ISLE corpus of non-native spoken English". In: *Proc. LREC*, pp. 957–963, Athens, Greece, 2000.

[Mich 99]   B. Michiels. "Die Rolle der Niederländischkenntnisse bei französischsprachigen Lernern von Deutsch als L3". *Zeitschrift für Interkulturellen Fremdsprachenunterricht*, 1999.

[Mine 02]   N. Minematsu, Y. Tomiyama, K. Yoshimoto, K. Shimizu, S. Nakagawa, M. Dantsuji, and S. Makino. "English speech database read by Japanese learners for CALL system development". In: *Proc. LREC*, pp. 896–903, Las Palmas, Spain, 2002.

[Mink 04]   W. Minker and S. Bennacef. *Speech and Human-Machine Dialog*. Kluwer Academic Publishers, Boston, USA, 2004.

[Morg 04]   J. Morgan. "Making a speech recognizer tolerate non-native speech through Gaussian mixture merging". In: *Proc. InSTIL*, p. no pagination, Venice, Italy, 2004.

[Morg 06]   J. Morgan. "West Point heroico Spanish speech". Tech. Rep., LDC, Philadelphia, USA, 2006.

[Mote 04]   N. Mote, L. Johnson, A. Sethy, J. Silva, and S. Narayanan. "Tactical language detection and modeling of learner speech errors: The case of Arabic tactical language training for American English speakers". In: *Proc. InSTIL*, Venice, Italy, June 2004.

[Nems 71]   W. Nemser. "Approximative systems for foreign language learners". *International Review of Applied Linguistics*, pp. 115–123, 1971.

[Nguy 99]   P. Nguyen, P. Gelin, J.-C. Junqua, and J.-T. Chien. "N-Best based supervised and unsupervised adaptation for native and non-native speakers in cars". In: *Proc. ICASSP*, pp. 173–176, Phoenix, USA, 1999.

[Nies 06]   T. Niesler. "Language-dependent state clustering for multilingual speech recognition in Afrikaans, South African English, Xhosa and Zulu". In: *Proc. ITRW*, Stellenbosch, South Africa, 2006.

[Nish 04]   K. Nishina. "Development of Japanese speech database read by non-native speakers for constructing CALL system". In: *Proc. ICA*, pp. 561–564, Kyoto, Japan, 2004.

[Noor 09]   G. Noord. "TextCat". 2009. http://odur.let.rug.nl/~vannoord/TextCat/.

[Noth 91]   E. Nöth. *Prosodische Information in der automatischen Spracherkennung. Berechnung und Anwendung*. Niemeyer, Tüebingen, Germany, 1991.

[Onom 95]   Onomastica Consortium. "The ONOMASTICA interlanguage pronunciation lexicon". In: *Proc. Eurospeech*, pp. 829–832, Madrid, Spain, 1995.

[Pete 08]   K. Petersen and M. Pedersen. "The matrix cookbook". 2008. http://matrixcookbook.com.

[Pige 07]   S. Pigeon, W. Shen, and D. van Leeuwen. "Design and characterization of the non-native military air traffic communications database". In: *Proc. Interspeech*, Antwerp, Belgium, 2007.

[Plat 88]   J. C. Platt and A. H. Bar. "Constrained differential optimization for neural networks". Tech. Rep., Caltech, USA, 1988.

[Raab 04]   M. Raab. *Co-operative learning in mathematics - An attempt to foster asynchronous co-operation via email in higher education*. Studienarbeit, Institut für Algorithmen und Kognitive Systeme, Universität Karlsruhe, Karlsruhe, Germany, 2004.

[Raab 06] M. Raab. *Language modeling for machine translation*. Diplomarbeit, Institut für Theoretische Informatik, Universität Karlsruhe, Karlsruhe, Germany, 2006.

[Raab 07a] M. Raab. *Language modeling for machine translation*. Vdm Verlag, Saarbruecken, Germany, 2007.

[Raab 07b] M. Raab, R. Gruhn, and E. Nöth. "Non-native speech databases". In: *Proc. ASRU*, pp. 413–418, Kyoto, Japan, 2007.

[Raab 08a] M. Raab. "Non-native speech databases". 2008. http://en.wikipedia.org/wiki/Non-native_speech_databases.

[Raab 08b] M. Raab, R. Gruhn, and E. Nöth. "Codebook design for speech guided car infotainment systems". In: *Proc. PIT*, pp. 44–51, Kloster Irsee, Germany, 2008.

[Raab 08c] M. Raab, R. Gruhn, and E. Nöth. "Multilingual weighted codebooks". In: *Proc. ICASSP*, pp. 4257–4260, Las Vegas, USA, 2008.

[Raab 08d] M. Raab, R. Gruhn, and E. Nöth. "Multilingual weighted codebooks for non-native speech recognition". In: *Proc. TSD*, pp. 485–492, Brno, Czech Republic, 2008.

[Raab 08e] M. Raab, T. Herbig, R. Brückner, R. Gruhn, and E. Nöth. "Adaptation of frequency band influence for non-native speech recognition". In: *Proc. ESSV*, pp. 149–156, Frankfurt, Germany, 2008.

[Raab 09a] M. Raab, G. Aradilla, R. Gruhn, and E. Nöth. "Online generation of acoustic models for multilingual speech recognition". In: *Proc. Interspeech*, pp. 2999–3002, Brighton, UK, 2009.

[Raab 09b] M. Raab, R. Gruhn, and E. Nöth. "Multilingual speech interfaces for resource-constrained dialog systems". In: *Proc. IWSDS*, Kloster Irsee, Germany, 2009.

[Raab 09c] M. Raab, O. Schreiner, T. Herbig, R. Gruhn, and E. Nöth. "Optimal projections between Gaussian mixture feature spaces for multilingual speech recognition". In: *Proc. DAGA*, pp. 411–414, Rotterdam, Netherlands, 2009.

[Rabi 89] L. R. Rabiner. "A tutorial on hidden Markov models and selected applications in speech recognition". *Proc. of the IEEE*, Vol. 77, 1989.

[Reyn 95] D. A. Reynolds. "Large population speaker identification using clean and telephone speech". *IEEE Signal Process. Lett.*, pp. 44–48, 1995.

[Rhee 04] S.-C. Rhee, S.-H. Lee, S.-K. Kang, and Y.-J. Lee. "Design and construction of Korean-spoken English corpus(K-SEC)". In: *Proc. Interspeech*, pp. 2769–2772, Jeju Island, Korea, 2004.

[Rose 00] R. Rosenfeld. "Two decades of statistical language modeling: where do we go from here?". *Proc. of the IEEE*, 2000.

[Scha 06a] S. Schaden. "Casselberveetovallarga and other unpronounceable places: The CrossTowns corpus". In: *Proc. LREC*, pp. 993–998, Genoa, Italy, 2006.

[Scha 06b] S. Schaden. *Regelbasierte Modellierung fremdsprachlich akzentbehafteter Aussprachevarianten.* PhD thesis, University Duisburg-Essen, Duisburg, Germnay, 2006.

[Schu 00] T. Schultz and A. Waibel. "Experiments towards a multi-language LVCSR interface". In: *Proc. Interspeech*, pp. 129–132, Bejing, China, 2000.

[Schu 01] T. Schultz and A. Waibel. "Language-independent and language-adaptive acoustic modeling for speech recognition". *Speech Communication*, Vol. 35, pp. 31–51, 2001.

[Schu 06] T. Schultz and K. Kirchhoff. *Multilingual speech processing.* Academic Press, 2006.

[Schu 99] T. Schultz and A. Waibel. "Language adaptive LVCSR through Polyphone Decision Tree Specialization". In: *Proc. MIST*, pp. 85–90, Leusden, The Netherlands, 1999.

[Segu 07] J. Segura, T. Ehrette, A. Potamianos, D. Fohr, I. Illina, P.-A. Breton, V. Clot, R. Gemello, M. Matassoni, and P. Maragos. "The HIWIRE database, a noisy and non-native English speech corpus for cockpit communication". 2007. http://www.hiwire.org/.

[Seli 72] L. Selinker. "Interlanguage". *International Review of Applied Linguistics*, pp. 209–231, 1972.

[Spee 02] Speech Resources Consortium. "UME-ERJ English speech database read by Japanese students". 2002. http://research.nii.ac.jp/src/eng/list/index.html.

[Stei 04] S. Steidl, G. Stemmer, C. Hacker, and E. Nöth. "Adaption in the pronunciation space for non-native speech recognition". In: D. Kim, S. and Youn, Ed., *Proc. Interspeech*, pp. 318–321, Jeju Island, Korea, 2004.

[Stem 01] G. Stemmer, E. Nöth, and H. Niemann. "Acoustic modeling of foreign words in a German speech recognition system". In: P. Dalsgaard, B. Lindberg, and H. Benner, Eds., *Proc. Interspeech*, pp. 2745–2748, 2001.

[Stue 03a] S. Stueker, F. Metze, T. Schultz, and A. Waibel. "Integrating multilingual articulatory features into speech recognition". In: *Proc. Interspeech*, pp. 1033–1036, Geneva, Switzerland, 2003.

[Stue 03b] S. Stueker, T. Schultz, F. Metze, and A. Waibel. "Multilingual articulatory features". In: *Proc. ICASSP*, pp. 144–147, Hong Kong, China, 2003.

[Stue 06] S. Stueker, C. Fuegen, R. Hsiao, S. Ikbal, Q. Jin, F. Kraft, M. Paulik, M. Raab, Y. Tam, and M.Woelfel. "The ISL TC-STAR spring 2006 ASR evaluation systems". In: *Proc. of the TC-STAR Workshop on Speech-to-Speech Translation*, Barcelona, Spain, 2006.

[Sun 98] Sun Microsystems. *Java Speech Grammar Format Specification.* Sun Microsystems, 1998.

[Tan 06] T. P. Tan and L. Besacier. "A French non-native corpus for automatic speech recognition". In: *Proc. LREC*, pp. 1610–1613, Genoa, Italy, 2006.

[Tan 07a] T. P. Tan and L. Besacier. "Acoustic model interpolation for non-native speech recognition". In: *Proc. ICASSP*, pp. 1009–1013, Honolulu, Hawaii, 2007.

[Tan 07b] T. P. Tan and L. Besacier. "Modeling context and language variation for non-native speech variation". In: *Proc. Interspeech*, pp. 1429–1432, Antwerp, Belgium, 2007.

[Tan 08] T. P. Tan. *Reconnaissance de la parole multilingue : application au malais.* PhD thesis, CLIPS-IMAG, Grenoble, France, 2008.

[Teix 97] C. Teixeira, I. Trancoso, and A. Serralheiro. "Recognition of non-native accents". In: *Proc. Eurospeech*, pp. 2375–2378, Rhodes, Greece, 1997.

[TNO 07] TNO Human Factors Research Institute. "MIST multi-lingual interoperability in speech technology database". Tech. Rep., TNO Human Factors Research Institute, Paris, France, 2007. ELRA Catalog Reference S0238.

[Tomo 01a] L. M. Tomokiyo. *Recognizing non-native speech: characterizing and adapting to non-native usage in speech recognition.* PhD thesis, Carnegie Mellon University, Pittsburgh, USA, 2001.

[Tomo 01b] L. M. Tomokiyo and A. Waibel. "Adaptation methods for non-native speech". In: *Proc. MSLP*, pp. 39–44, Aalborg, Denmark, 2001.

[Tran 99] I. Trancoso, C. Viana, I. Mascarenhas, and C. Teixeira. "On deriving rules for nativised pronunciation in navigation queries". In: *Proc. Eurospeech*, pp. 195–198, Budapest, Hungary, 1999.

[Uebl 01] U. Uebler. "Multilingual speech recognition in seven languages". *Speech Communication*, Vol. 35, pp. 53–69, 2001.

[Ueda 90] Y. Ueda and S. Nakagawa. "Prediction for phoneme/syllable/word-category and identification of language using HMM". In: *Proc. ICSLP*, pp. 1209–1212, Kobe, Japan, 1990.

[Univ 98] University Munich. "Bavarian archive for speech signals Strange Corpus". 1998. http://www.phonetik.uni-muenchen.de/Bas/BasSC1eng.html.

[Wahl 00] W. Wahlster. *Verbmobil: Foundations of speech-to-speech translation.* Springer, 2000.

[Wang 03] Z. Wang, T. Schultz, and A. Waibel. "Comparison of acoustic model adaptation techniques on non-native speech". In: *Proc. ICASSP*, pp. 540–543, Hong Kong, China, 2003.

[Ward 98] T. Ward, S. Roukos, C. Neti, J. Gros, M. Epstein, and S. Dharanipragada. "Towards speech understanding across multiple languages". In: *Proc. ICSLP*, p. no pagination, Sydney, Australia, 1998.

[Well 08] J. Wells. "SAMPA". 2008. http://www.phon.ucl.ac.uk/home/sampa/.

[Weng 97] F. Weng, H. Bratt, L. Neumeyer, and A. Stolcke. "A study of multilingual speech recognition". In: *Proc. Eurospeech*, pp. 359–362, Rhodes, Greece, 1997.

[Witt 99a] S. Witt. *Use of speech recognition in computer-assisted language learning.* PhD thesis, Cambridge University Engineering Department, Cambridge, UK, 1999.

[Witt 99b]   S. Witt and S. Young. "Off-line acoustic modeling of non-native accents". In: *Proc. Eurospeech*, pp. 1367–1370, Budapest, Hungary, 1999.

[Xu 98]   W. Xu, J. Duchateau, K. Demuynck, and I. Dologlou. "A new approach to merging Gaussian densities in large vocabulary continous speech recognition". In: *Proc. IEEE Benelux Signal Processing Symposium*, pp. 231–234, Leuven, Belgium, 1998.

[Ye 05]   H. Ye and S. Young. "Improving the speech recognition performance of beginners in spoken conversational interaction for language learning". In: *Proc. Interspeech*, pp. 289–292, Lisbon, Portugal, 2005.

[Yi 06]   L. Yi and P. Fu. "Multi-accent Chinese speech recognition". In: *Proc. Interspeech*, pp. 133–136, Pittsburgh, USA, 2006.